WHALES

Diving into the Unknown

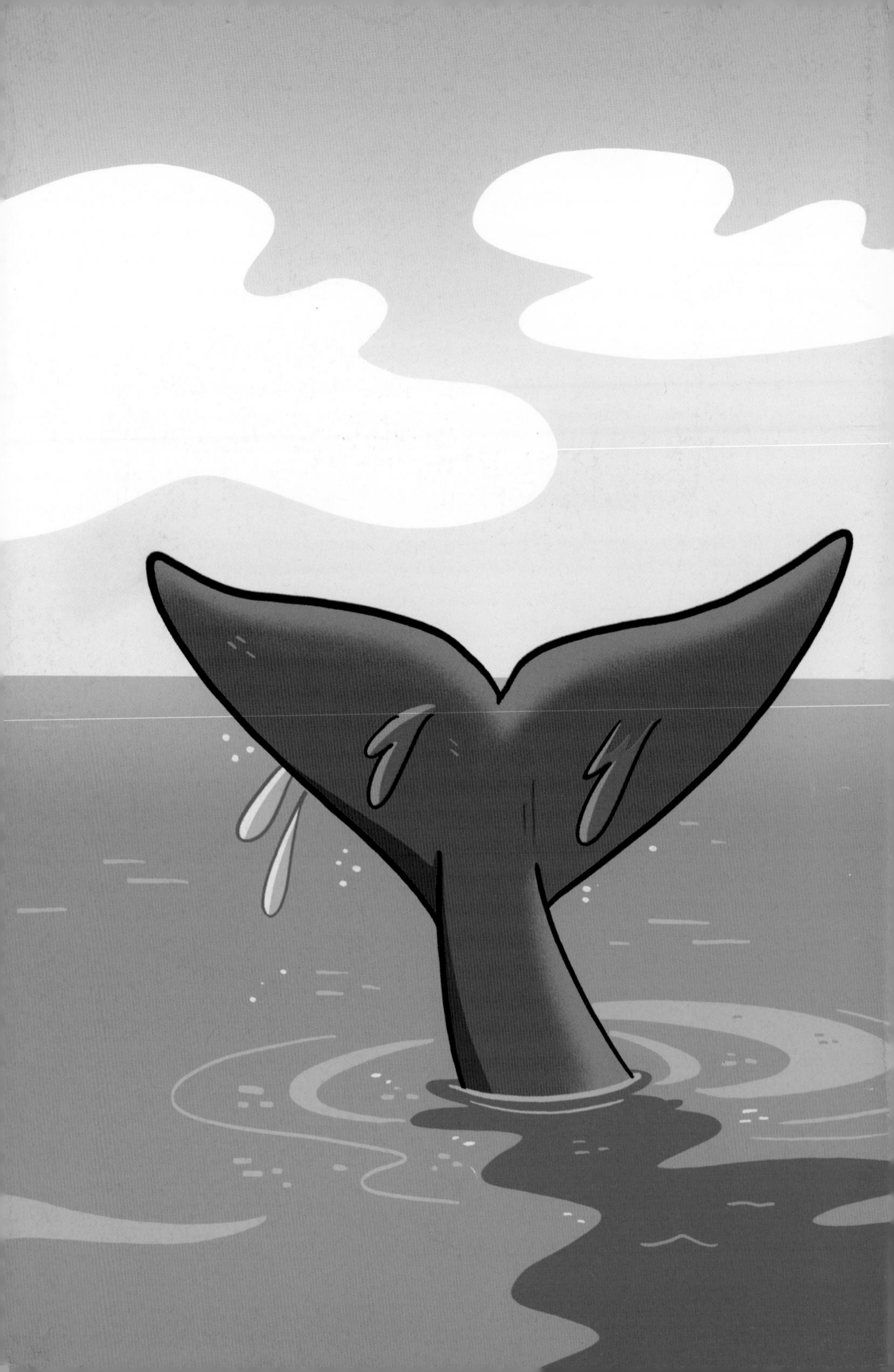

WHALES
Diving into the Unknown

written by
Casey Zakroff
art by
Pat Lewis

:01

First Second

New York

First Second

Published by First Second
First Second is an imprint of Roaring Brook Press,
 a division of Holtzbrinck Publishing Holdings Limited Partnership
120 Broadway, New York, NY 10271
firstsecondbooks.com
mackids.com

Library of Congress Control Number: 2021904058

Our books may be purchased in bulk for promotional, educational, or business use. Please
contact your local bookseller or the Macmillan Corporate and Premium Sales Department
at (800) 221-7945 ext. 5442 or by email at MacmillanSpecialMarkets@macmillan.com.

FIRST
EDITION

First edition, 2021
Edited by Dave Roman
Cover and interior book design by Sunny Lee
Whales consultant: Annamaria DeAngelis

Penciled on Strathmore 300 series vellum Bristol paper with a Staedler Mars Technico 2mm lead holder.
Inked and colored digitally in Photoshop using a Windows Surface pen.

Printed in China by Toppan Leefung Printing Ltd., Dongguan City, Guangdong Province

ISBN 978-1-250-22838-3 (paperback)
10 9 8 7 6 5 4 3 2 1

ISBN 978-1-250-22839-0 (hardcover)
10 9 8 7 6 5 4 3 2 1

Don't miss your next favorite book from First Second! For the latest updates go to firstsecondnewsletter.com
and sign up for our enewsletter.

I grew up dreaming of becoming an adventurer scientist—someone who would go where no one else would ever go and see what no one else would ever see. As a child, I fell in love with water of any kind—as long as I could lie in it till my fingers became prune-like. Even though I come from the beautiful tropical island of Sri Lanka, located in the heart of the Indian Ocean, I did not grow up in a family that went on vacation to the beach. It was just not something we did. However, from the top of the hill where we lived, I would see the ocean every day on my way to school. I knew there were untold secrets lurking beneath the waves, and I was convinced it was not just a big, blue tank of water but that if I lifted the lid and looked inward, it would be a portal to a magical kingdom. Fast forward to today and I KNOW that I was right.

But somewhere between my childhood and university, something clicked. I realized I could hold on to and grow my dream of becoming an adventurer scientist if I became a marine biologist. It had all the ingredients I needed—adventure, science, and salty water. By the time I was ready to go to university, I knew what I would study—the ocean and its many unraveled mysteries. It wasn't necessarily straightforward, though. My island, also known as the pearl of the Indian Ocean, is beautiful and tropical, but most people had never heard of a marine biologist. Anyone who worked with the ocean was a fisherperson rather than a scientist or conservationist, and here I was telling them I wanted to not just study it but also look after it! Long story short, I had to prove myself to them, and in the process I discovered the secrets of a unique, non-migratory population of blue whales before anyone took me seriously.

My first foray into scientific research was with sperm whales. I was studying their acoustics and learning about how similar they are to elephants. I come from a country where we have both species, so my mind began whizzing!

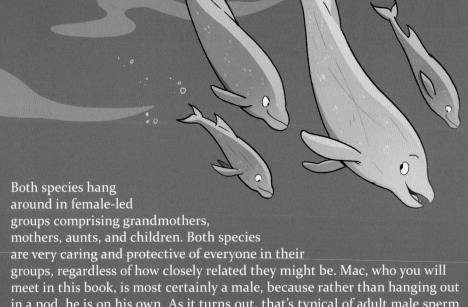

Both species hang around in female-led groups comprising grandmothers, mothers, aunts, and children. Both species are very caring and protective of everyone in their groups, regardless of how closely related they might be. Mac, who you will meet in this book, is most certainly a male, because rather than hanging out in a pod, he is on his own. As it turns out, that's typical of adult male sperm whales, and even elephants. Once they mature, they break away from their family groups and do their own thing or hang around with other boys!

That first piece of research definitely led me to believe that I would dedicate my life to whales despite the fact that I had never seen one. Lucky for me, I got the opportunity to spend more time with them not too long after I finished my undergraduate degree. I was a deckhand (cleaning toilets and polishing brass) on a research vessel that was tracking sperm whales around the northern Indian Ocean. Surrounded by sperm whales every day, hearing their cacophonous sounds through the loudspeakers aboard our vessel was enough to further solidify my yearning to work with these square-headed, elusive beasts long-term. That was, of course, until I encountered an aggregation of blue whales and a floating pile of whale poop. Not many people can say their careers started with a pile of poop, but mine did—because that was my eureka moment, and that's the moment I launched the first-ever long-term research project on blue whales within the northern Indian Ocean.

Fast forward to today: I have done a lot of things, particularly with blue whales and sperm whales, but everything has a single focus—conservation. A lot of people think I work with whales because they are amazing to watch, but in reality that's just half the story. Along the way, I have learned how important they are to keeping us alive. In a nutshell, whales feed at the depths of our oceans, then come up to the surface to poop. Scientists call these giant plumes *poo-nadoes* because there's just so much of it and it does come out with a fair amount of force! This poop is full of nutrients that are the fertilizer for our oceans. It fertilizes the microscopic plants called *phytoplankton* that float across the surface of our oceans and feast on sunshine and nutrients that then enable them to photosynthesize and produce oxygen. Did you know that 50–70% of the oxygen we breathe is created by plants in the ocean? I am not trying to justify my love for poop, but really, whale poop is pretty important to all our lives!

Dedicating my life to whales has allowed me to live my childhood dream— go where no one else would ever go and see what no one else would ever see, while also allowing me the privilege to help look after them. This book does something similar but for a broader audience. It allows anyone who picks this book up to explore species and concepts, spaces and places, that will draw more people into the oceans.

No matter what challenges come my way, I feel continually grateful for the life I lead, the adventures I go on, and the wild spaces I see.

Asha de Vos, PhD
marine biologist and ocean educator
founder/executive director, Oceanswell, Sri Lanka

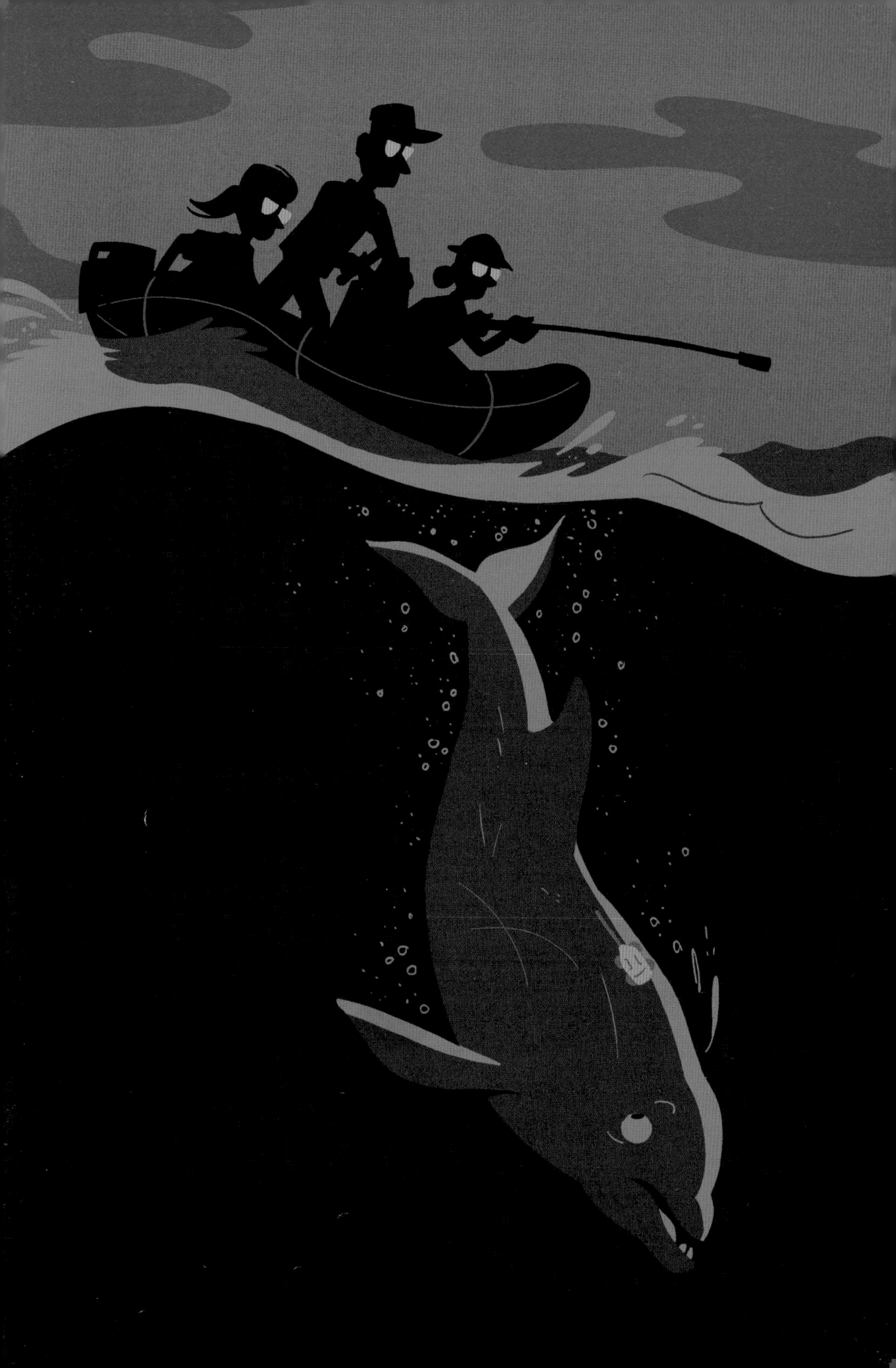

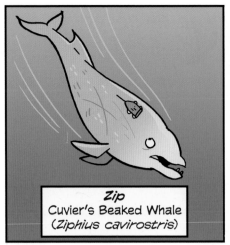

Zip
Cuvier's Beaked Whale
(*Ziphius cavirostris*)

Teut
Longfin Inshore Squid
(*Doryteuthis pealeii*)

PSHOO!

Aaaaah!

GASP

Aaaah!

Made first contact. Alien device attached to body. *Help!*

SNORT

Uh. Hello?

HAR HAR HAR

Whoa!

Can you help me? I'm turning into an alien cyborg!

Nothing so strange as that, young beaked whale. You've been adorned with a hydrophone!

Nova
Humpback Whale
(*Megaptera novaeangliae*)

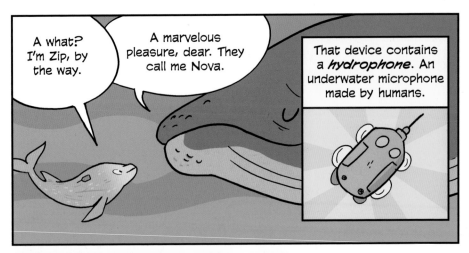

A what? I'm Zip, by the way.

A marvelous pleasure, dear. They call me Nova.

That device contains a *hydrophone*. An underwater microphone made by humans.

Humans? The aliens? Why would they stick a microphone on me?

To hear what you have to say, of course! The sounds you make!

I'm just a regular whale. Nothin' I have to say is so important that aliens would care about it.

Nonsense, lad! What you have to say is key to who you are!

Sound is everything to a whale!

What even is sound anyway?

Sound is a wave made when something vibrates.

Waves are a way that energy moves through matter, through the molecules that make up our bodies and all the stuff around us.

BAM!

Energy can't be made or destroyed, but can move through things, and things get excited—they move—when they have energy.

When molecules vibrate, they hit their neighbors and pass their energy onto them.

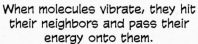

Woo!

Woo!

Woo!

The molecules rest until the next part of the wave moves through, and the process repeats until the energy wave passes or the energy is lost.

Lost?

A little bit of energy is always lost over time, so the sound eventually dies out, but how far it goes depends on how much energy the sound started with and what it is traveling through.

Sound travels faster, and farther, in matter where the molecules are more tightly packed or have stronger bonds, because the energy transfers more quickly and easily.

SLAP!

So the same sound will travel way farther and way faster in water than it will in air!

So sound is important because it allows us to communicate over long distances underwater, right?

Partly, yes!

But what are we vibrating to make sound?

In toothed whales like you, sound can be made by vibrating tissue in the *larynx* or by passing air through a set of *phonic lips* that vibrate in an air cavity beneath the *blowhole*.

BLOWHOLE
PHONIC LIPS
LARYNX

Most of you have two sets of lips so you can make two different sounds at the same time!

Baleen whales, like me, don't have phonic lips. We have a sac attached to our *larynx* that has a fold of tissue that vibrates when we pass air across it.

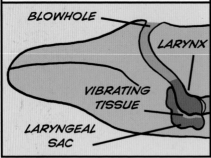

BLOWHOLE
LARYNX
VIBRATING TISSUE
LARYNGEAL SAC

Whales can finely control the air in our bodies to tune the types of sounds we make.

Clicks, whistles, grunts, squawks... Oh! And the songs, of course!

Wait, we're that different? Wait. What songs? Wait. This is crazy! How do you know all of this?

Sorry. I got excited and started asking too many questions.

Never be ashamed of your inquisitiveness, dear boy! Questions are how we make the unknown known!

HAR HAR HAR

My story also began by contact with strange alien devices...

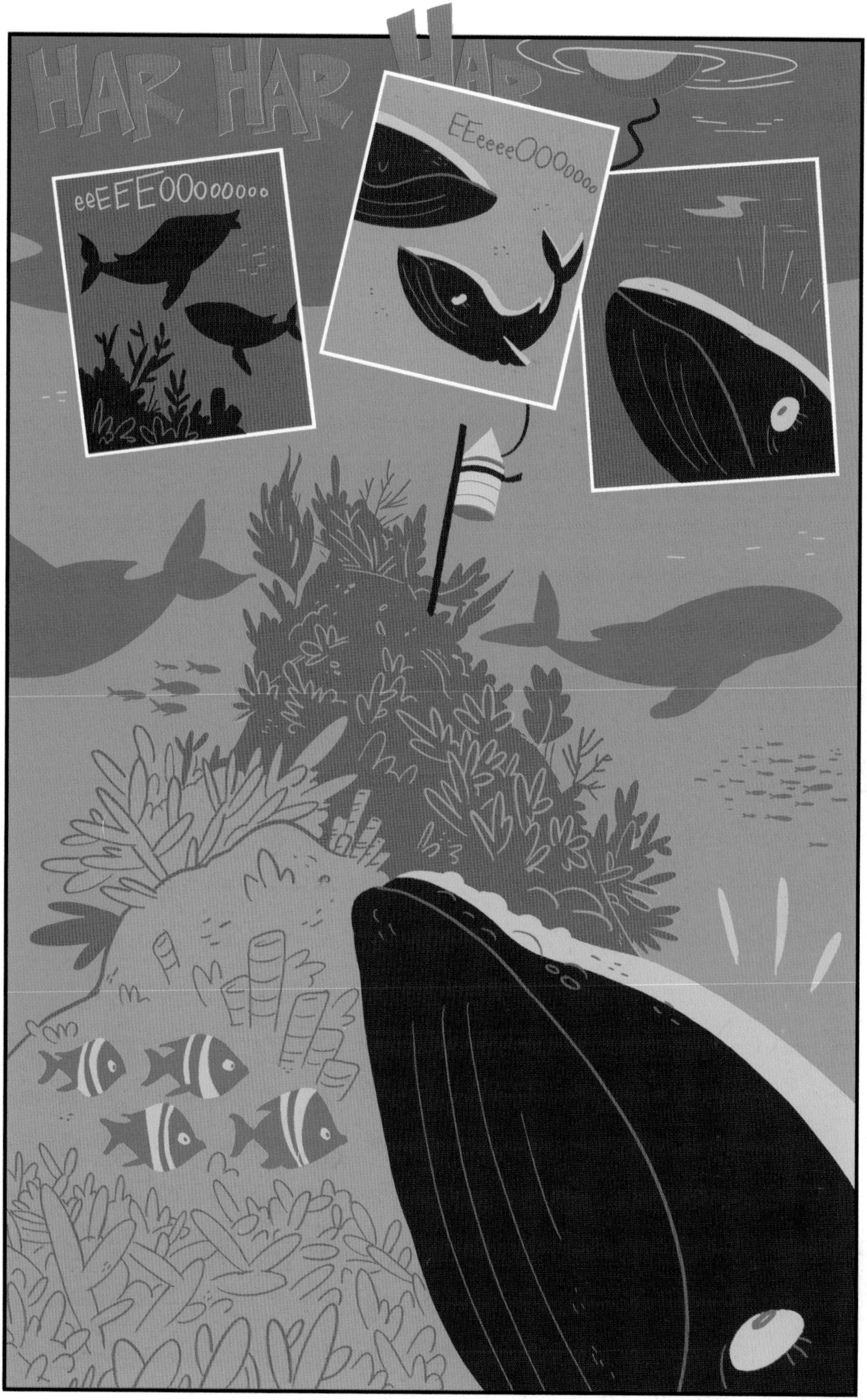
HAR HAR HAR
eeEEEOOoooooo
EEeeeeOOOoooo

What were the alien spires doing on the reef?!

Oh! Recording us, same as you! The hydrophones were just placed where we have our courtship rather than on our bodies.

Sound carries a lot of information. *Frequency*, measured in hertz (Hz), is how often a wave repeats in a second. This sets the pitch— what the sound sounds like.

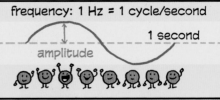

frequency: 1 Hz = 1 cycle/second

1 second

amplitude

The height of a sound wave, its *amplitude*, shows how much energy the sound has—how loud it is.

Putting all that information—that *data*— together, the aliens can draw our sounds and look at them, even a whole song!

Aliens can *see* sound?!

They take the *amplitude*—the energy— and paint with it. Louder sounds are brighter colors. How high they place the paint depends on the *frequency*—the pitch— and then they just draw along with time.

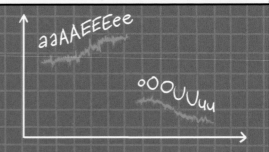

aaAAEEEee

ºOOUUuu

Whoa! So the aliens want to actually *see* what we have to *say*?!

Yes, de—

I can help with that! I know what to do now!!!

What do you me—

I'm going to make a *podcast!*

A what?

An audio recording with information for the aliens all about whales! Our pod! A podcast! *The Zip Files!*

That sounds lovely, Zip, but don't you think they want to hear about you? They attached the hydrophone to you.

I'm...I'm not all that interesting...

But talking to you has been great! And maybe other whales have made contact besides us! I can find them and talk to them!

Using the very tool the aliens gave you to learn more about them... I love it, lad!

What a grand adventure!

And I know just the whale for you to speak to first!

Just let me call him...

BOOSH!

Whoooa!

That was *so loud!*

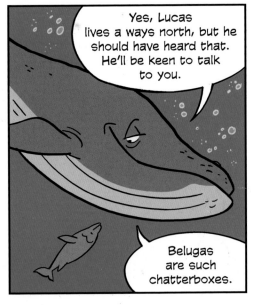

Yes, Lucas lives a ways north, but he should have heard that. He'll be keen to talk to you.

Belugas are such chatterboxes.

SLURRP

Hello!

Lucas
Beluga
(*Delphinapterus leucas*)

Finally found you!

I'd been spyhopping for a while, following your sound and keeping an eye out, and I saw Nova blow!

Ah, lovely!

Zip, this charming beluga is Lucas. Lucas, this young beaked whale is looking to—

Hi! Have you ever seen any aliens?!

Oh! Yeah! I was abducted and...

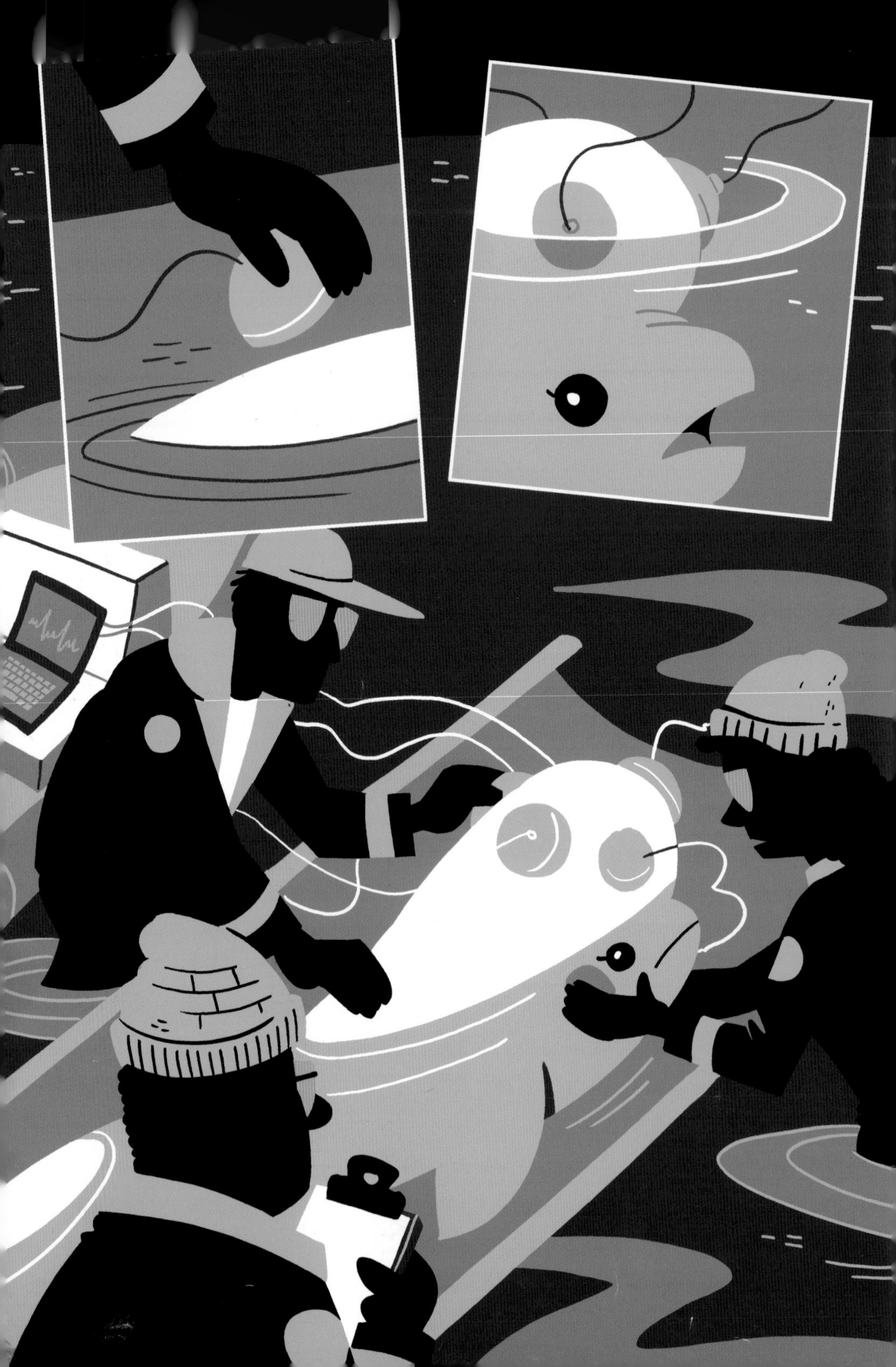

Whoa.
And you survived!
Were they recording
the sounds you
make?

They
let me go
after!

And no, they
wanted to see
how well I could
receive sound!

Receive sound? To hear?
Why would the aliens
be interested
in that?

Because sound
is everything to
a whale!

Sound is
both a physical
process and a
perception...

Sounds
don't mean very
much if you don't
have a way to
sense them!

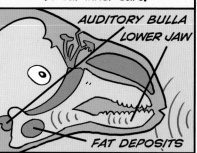

Whales like Zip and I pick up
sound vibrations through our
lower jaw and then transmit
them through deposits of fat
to our inner ears!

AUDITORY BULLA
LOWER JAW
FAT DEPOSITS

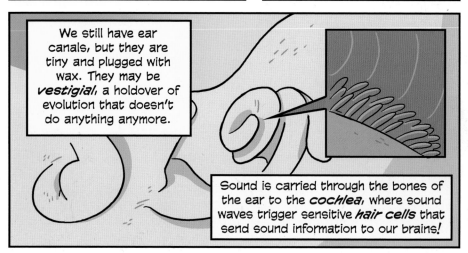

We still have ear
canals, but they are
tiny and plugged with
wax. They may be
vestigial, a holdover of
evolution that doesn't
do anything anymore.

Sound is carried through the bones of
the ear to the *cochlea*, where sound
waves trigger sensitive *hair cells* that
send sound information to our brains!

You both keep saying Nova is different from us. Nova, do you hear differently than we do?

Baleen whales are specialized to hear low-frequency sounds, while toothed whales are built for higher frequencies. My kind might hear through vibration of our skulls.

We don't really know! It hasn't been studied enough.

But how can we not know?

Zip, why do you think sound production and reception are so important for whales?

Hm...Sound travels really far underwater. Nova's breach was super loud...

Whales use sound to communicate with each other!

Even at long distances!

Yes, dear! And not just by slapping at the surface! We have a lot of *vocalizations*—sounds we use to communicate with each other.

CHIRP!
TRRRLL!
DING!

14

Baleen whales are specialized in making low-frequency sounds that sound like grunts or moans.

Frequency (Hz)

GROOOANN

Time

These sounds have high energy and can travel far, helping to coordinate whales over immense distances.

Males of some baleen whales organize sounds into patterns that they string together into longer, repeating calls, called *songs*.

Whales sing more during courtship than any other time, but it is still unclear exactly what the songs are for.

Frequency (Hz)

BWA-EE   BWA-EE

Toothed whales specialize in higher-frequency sounds.

We make a lot of short bursts of sound, often quickly repeating them as *pulsed calls.*

Some pods have their own *dialects!* Unique sets of calls they use to talk to one another.

Frequency (Hz)

TWEE-OO-WIT

Whistles are generally higher frequency, more continuous sounds that often have sweeping shifts in frequency.

We use calls and whistles to identify and coordinate with other whales in our pods and to express social cues like aggression or fear.

The highest-frequency sounds we can make, *clicks*, are used for much more than communication.

What do you mean?

We use clicks to sense our environment—to avoid obstacles and find food—especially when the water is murky or dark.

We SEE sound, too?!

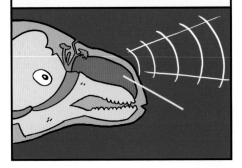

The *melon* is a structure in the front of our heads that focuses the sounds we make into a beam, like a flashlight.

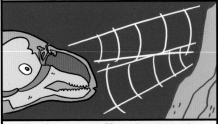

We send these focused, high-frequency sound waves to reflect off objects in the water and return to us.

We locate stuff by hearing the echoes of clicks: *echolocation!*

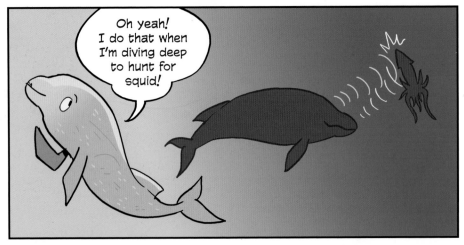

Oh yeah! I do that when I'm diving deep to hunt for squid!

Oh! I know an awesome squid hunter! You should interview him!

Whoa! Yeah! Let's go!

This is where your adventure begins in earnest, lad. Face the unknown head-on.

Ask questions. Listen and learn. And have fun!

It's a long swim over to his ocean, but I've always wanted to visit!

You haven't done this before? It's getting pretty cold...

...Are you sure we can do this?

Not normally, but it's warmer and there's less sea ice than there used to be, so I think we've got a shot!

FWOOSH

Oh! That's him!

Mac is a bit of a blowhard! I saw his blow over there!

His what?

The breath we exhale out of our *blowholes* when we surface is called *blow*.

We can't spray water out of our blowholes, but our breath is warm and moist. When it hits the cool air above us, water vapor in it condenses into a mist, like seeing your breath in winter!

Mac! Hey!

Lucas! Fancy seeing you in the Pacific! Who's the kid?

Mac
Sperm Whale
(*Physeter macrocephalus*)

I'm Zip! Lucas said you were a great squid hunter! I actual—

Oh ho! Here for a tale from a world-class diver, eh?

My record is 2,250 meters (7,380 feet) for 90 minutes!

See the secret, kid, is loading up on oxygen through big, deep breaths...

Yeah, I—

Our *blowholes* are our nostrils, kid. It's how whales breathe.

No water or food goes in or comes out of there! Air only.

Air comes in the blowhole passing our sound-producing structures and *larynx*, then enters the *trachea*, the tube connected to the lungs.

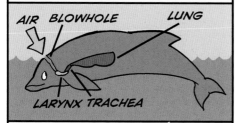

AIR   BLOWHOLE   LUNG

LARYNX TRACHEA

We have a lot of control of the air once it is inside us. We push it around to make all our sounds!

The lungs exchange oxygen in the air with carbon dioxide in the blood. Our blood is rich with a protein called *hemoglobin* that carries the oxygen to our muscles, where it is stored in another protein called *myoglobin*, which we whales have a ton of!

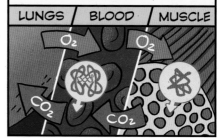

| LUNGS | BLOOD | MUSCLE |

O_2 O_2
CO_2 CO_2

I do that, too! I can dive deeper and longer than you, I think!

Oh ho! Then show me your stuff, kid!

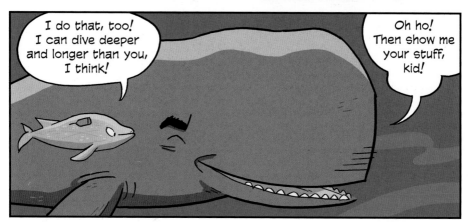

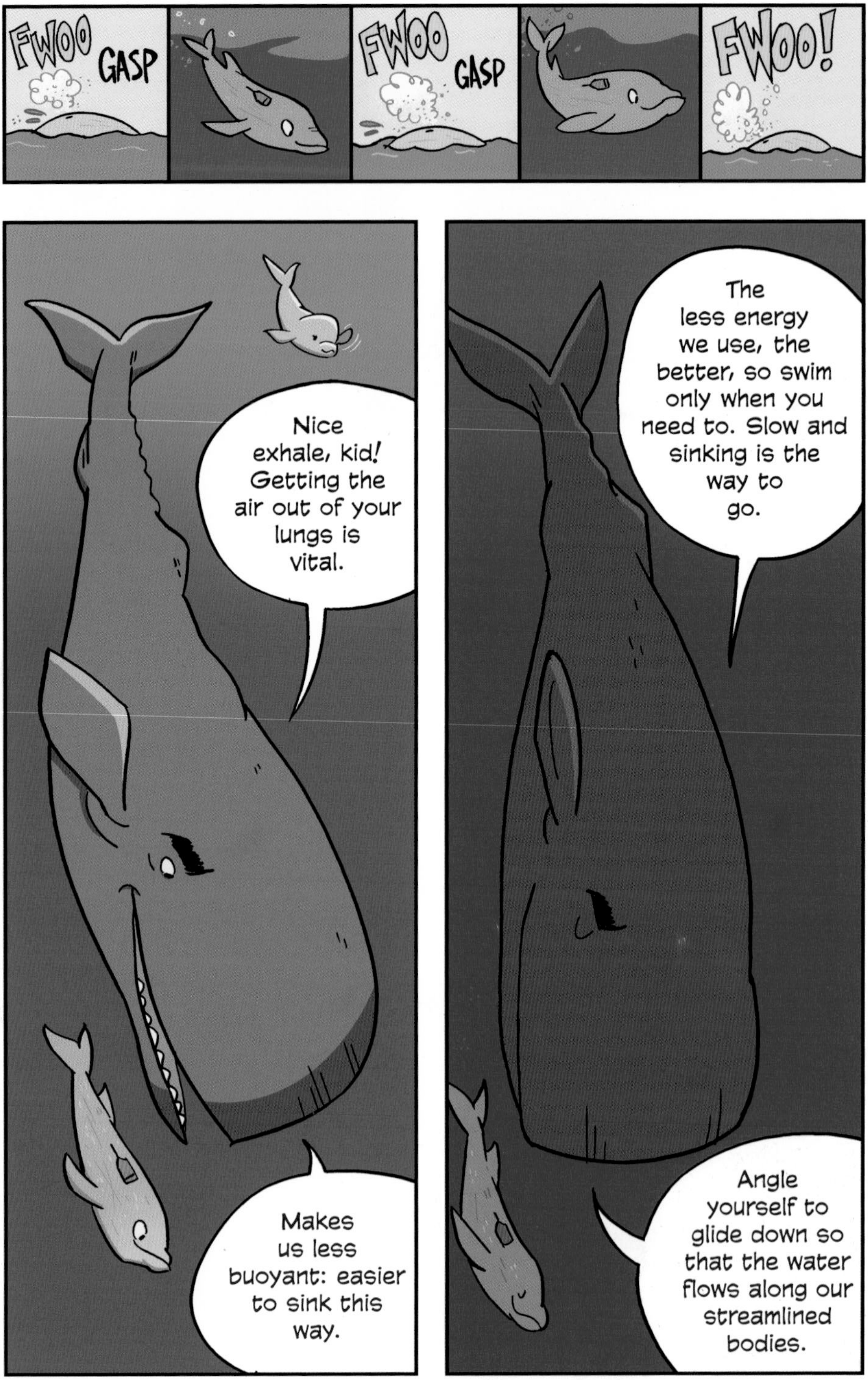

FWOO
GASP
FWOO
GASP
FWOO!
Nice exhale, kid! Getting the air out of your lungs is vital.
Makes us less buoyant: easier to sink this way.
The less energy we use, the better, so swim only when you need to. Slow and sinking is the way to go.
Angle yourself to glide down so that the water flows along our streamlined bodies.

Pressure increases as you go deeper in the ocean because there is more water on top of you pushing on your body.

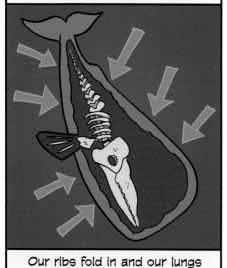

Our ribs fold in and our lungs collapse under the pressure.

Our bodies are surrounded by a thick layer of fat, *blubber*, to insulate us and keep us warm.

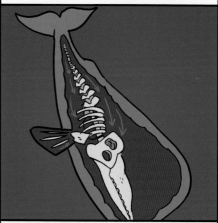

Blood is brought into our muscles and brains to conserve heat and oxygen. Our heart rate slows way down and we shut down all non-vital systems, like digestion.

And it gets darker as we get deeper, but you said you are used to this, right, kid?

Yeah, diving is my element.

Way easier than interviewing other whales...

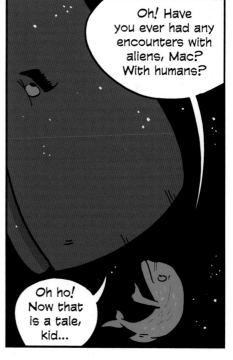

Oh! Have you ever had any encounters with aliens, Mac? With humans?

Oh ho! Now that is a tale, kid...

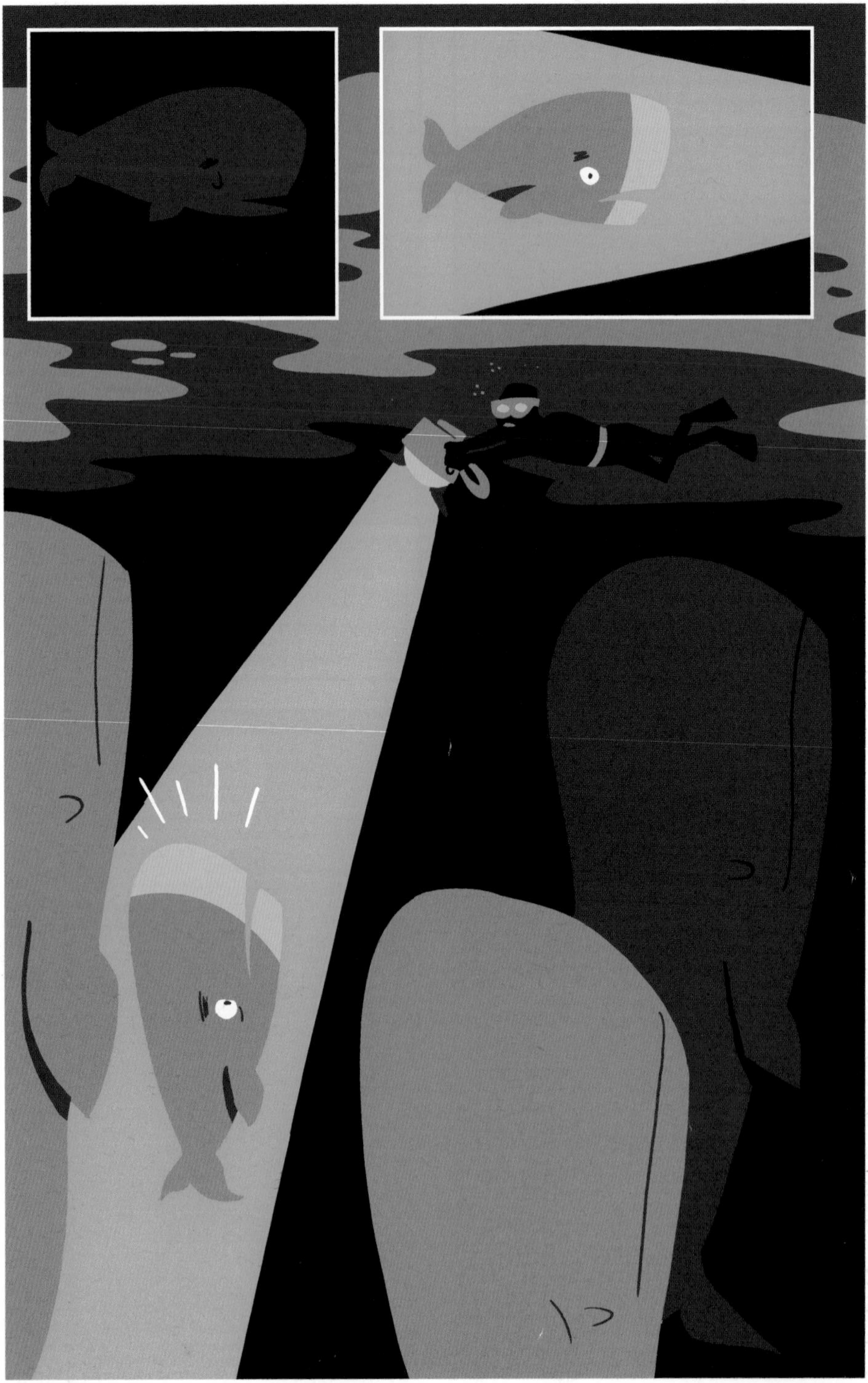

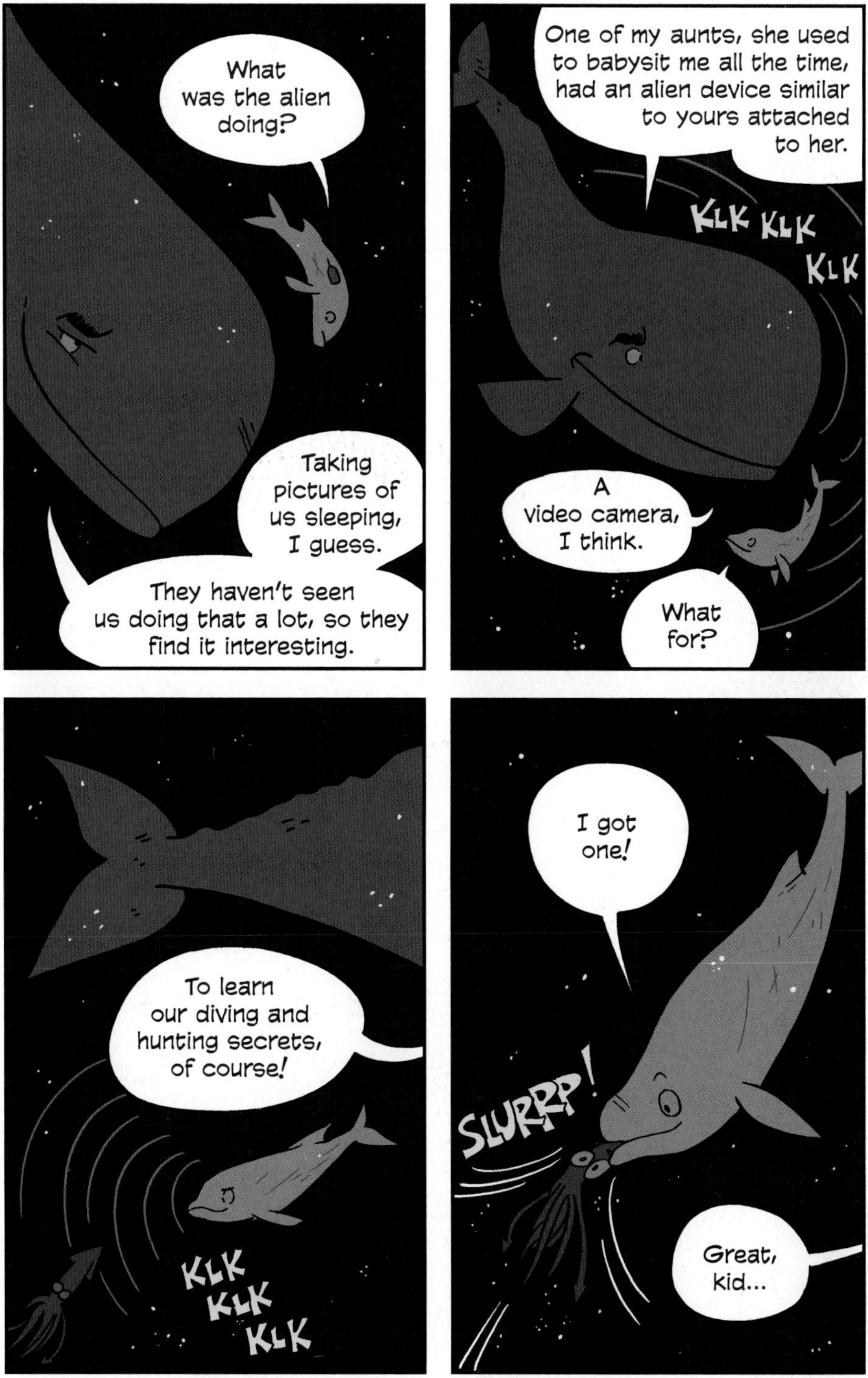
What was the alien doing?
Taking pictures of us sleeping, I guess.
They haven't seen us doing that a lot, so they find it interesting.
One of my aunts, she used to babysit me all the time, had an alien device similar to yours attached to her.
KLK KLK KLK
A video camera, I think.
What for?
To learn our diving and hunting secrets, of course!
KLK KLK KLK
I got one!
SLURRP!
Great, kid...

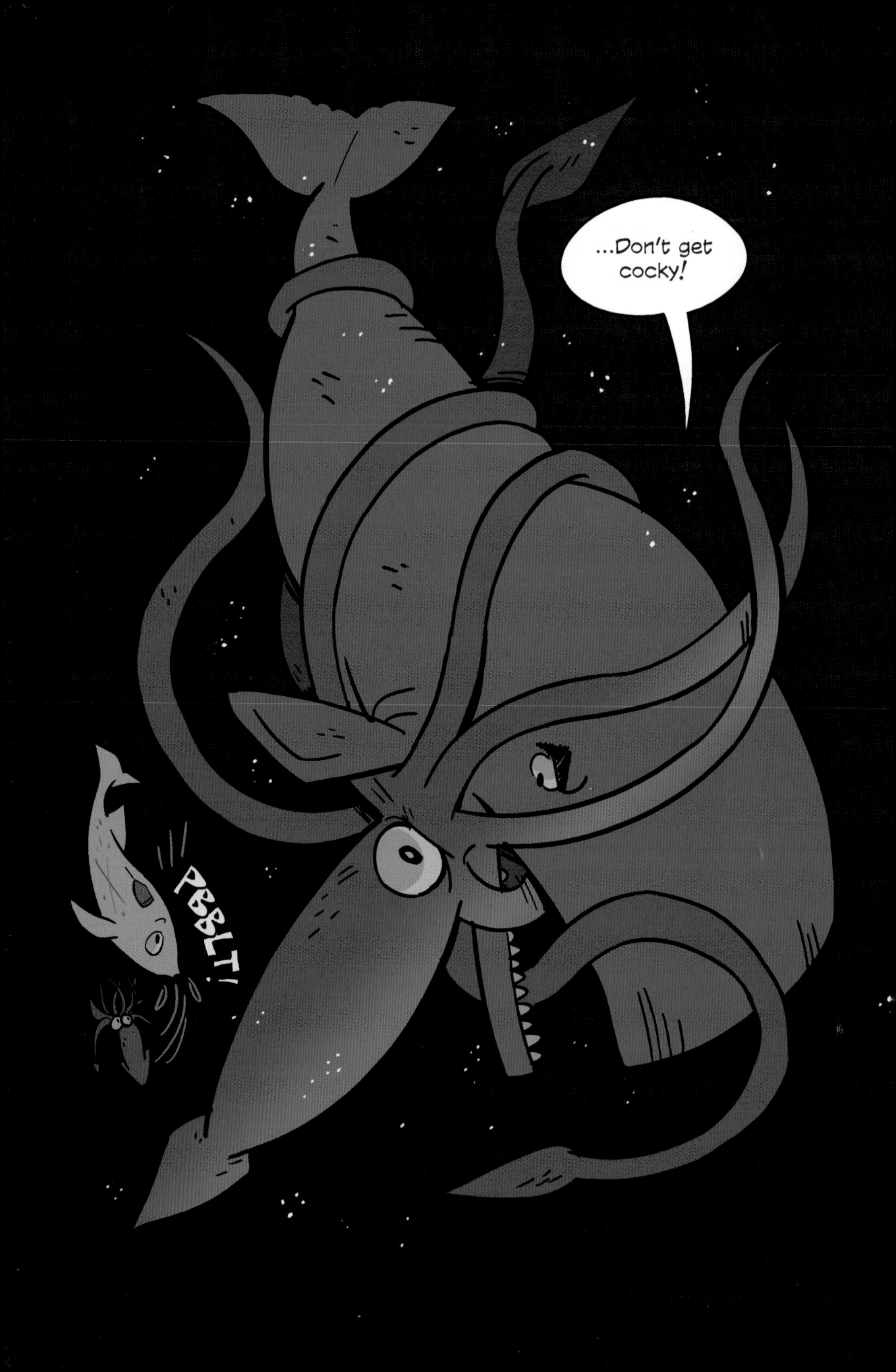
...Don't get
cocky!
PBBLT!

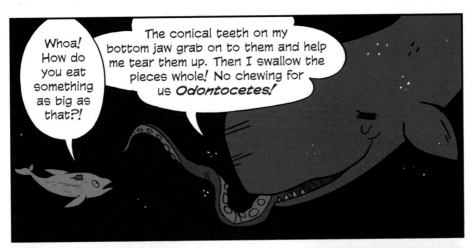

Whoa! How do you eat something as big as that?!

The conical teeth on my bottom jaw grab on to them and help me tear them up. Then I swallow the pieces whole! No chewing for us *Odontocetes!*

I just suck in my food. My teeth are mostly just for show...

Odonto-whats?

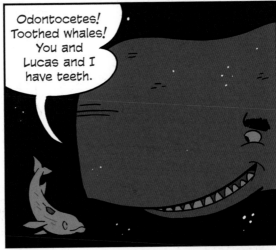

Odontocetes! Toothed whales! You and Lucas and I have teeth.

Oh! Right! That's one of the ways we were different from Nova!

Come on, kid...

...Let's head up.

You did good, kid. How deep'd you say you go?

My depth record is around 2,992 meters (9,816 feet).

On another dive, I was down for more than 3½ hours!

Oh ho! You really are an expert! You can tell me why we have to ascend carefully then, right?

Um, yeah! Yeah.

We don't want to get *decompression sickness—* the bends.

If we ascend too fast, pressure is released too quickly and gas bubbles can form in our blood, blocking blood flow and damaging organs.

Pressure decreasing slowly. Lungs expanding. Non-vital systems coming back online. Now to digest that meal, eh, kid!

Uh, yeah! Digest?

Our digestive system, how we eat, is separated from our respiratory system, how we breathe. Food, mostly swallowed whole, goes from the mouth, down the *esophagus*, and into the first chamber of our stomachs, where it can be stored for digestion.

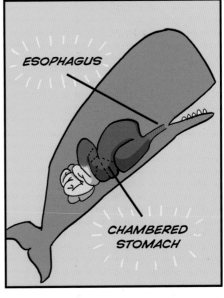

ESOPHAGUS

CHAMBERED STOMACH

Food is broken down mechanically in the forestomach, then by acid in the main stomach, and then processed through additional chambers before passing into the intestines for absorption.

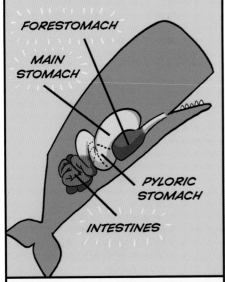

FORESTOMACH

MAIN STOMACH

PYLORIC STOMACH

INTESTINES

Anything we can't digest, like squid beaks, usually gets thrown back up.

Usually?

We sperm whales produce this waxy stuff in our intestines, *ambergris*, that coats indigestible stuff to help us poop it out.

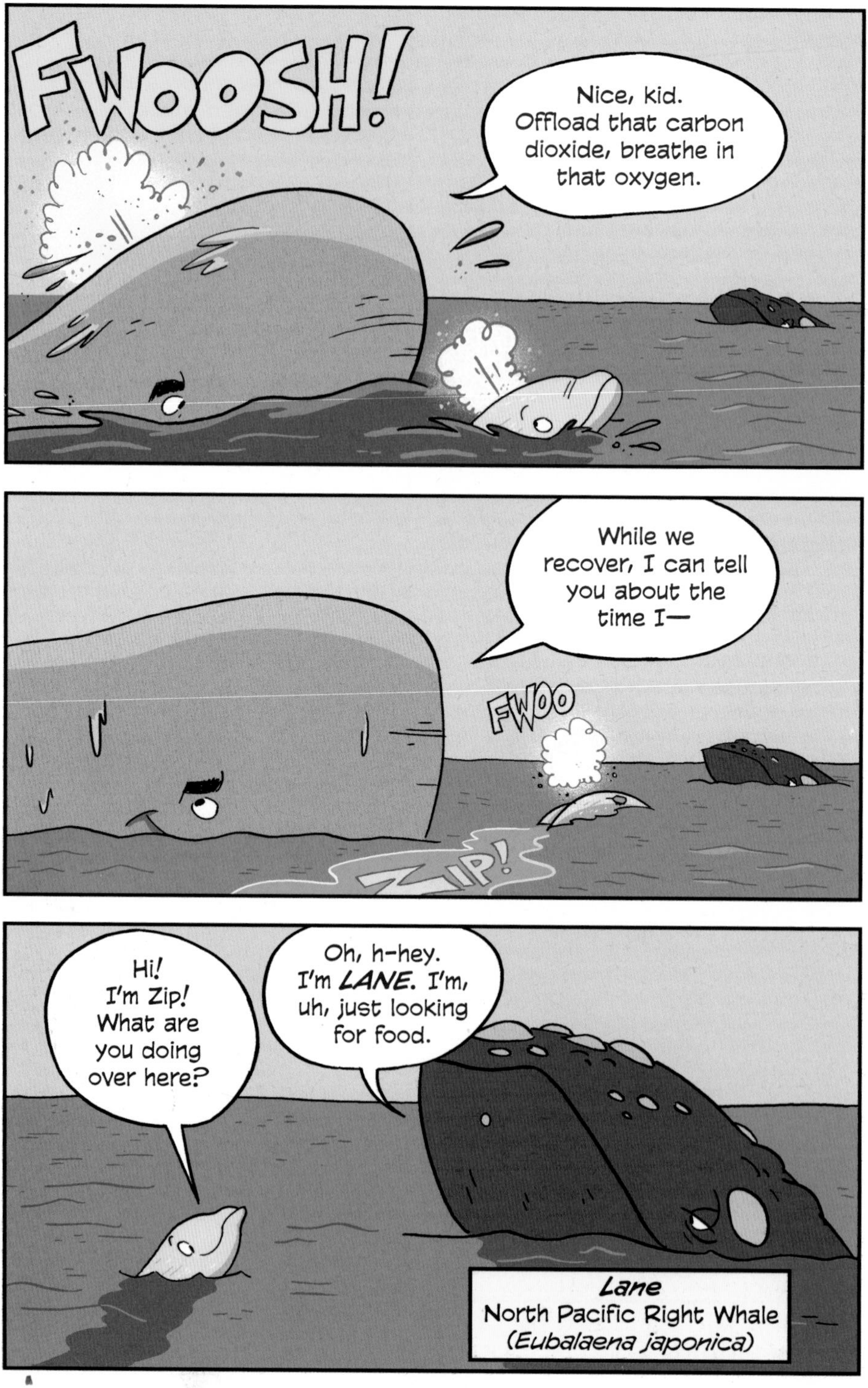
FWOOSH!
Nice, kid. Offload that carbon dioxide, breathe in that oxygen.
While we recover, I can tell you about the time I—
FWOO
ZIP!
Hi! I'm Zip! What are you doing over here?
Oh, h-hey. I'm LANE. I'm, uh, just looking for food.
Lane
North Pacific Right Whale
(Eubalaena japonica)

Oh, are you using echolocation?

No, us **MYSTICETES** don't really do that. We use our senses, like **SMELL**, to find patches of food. I've tracked schools of some kinds of fish from **HEARING** them **FARTING**...

Mysticetes? That means you are like Nova? Instead of teeth, you have baleen?

What **IS** baleen, anyway?

Baleen is what we call these **PLATES** that I use to filter-feed. It is made out of keratin, the same stuff as **HAIR**.

Why are you asking **ME** so many questions?

Oh! I'm making a podcast talking to whales that have made contact with aliens! Have—

OH! I've seen a **UFO** before!!!

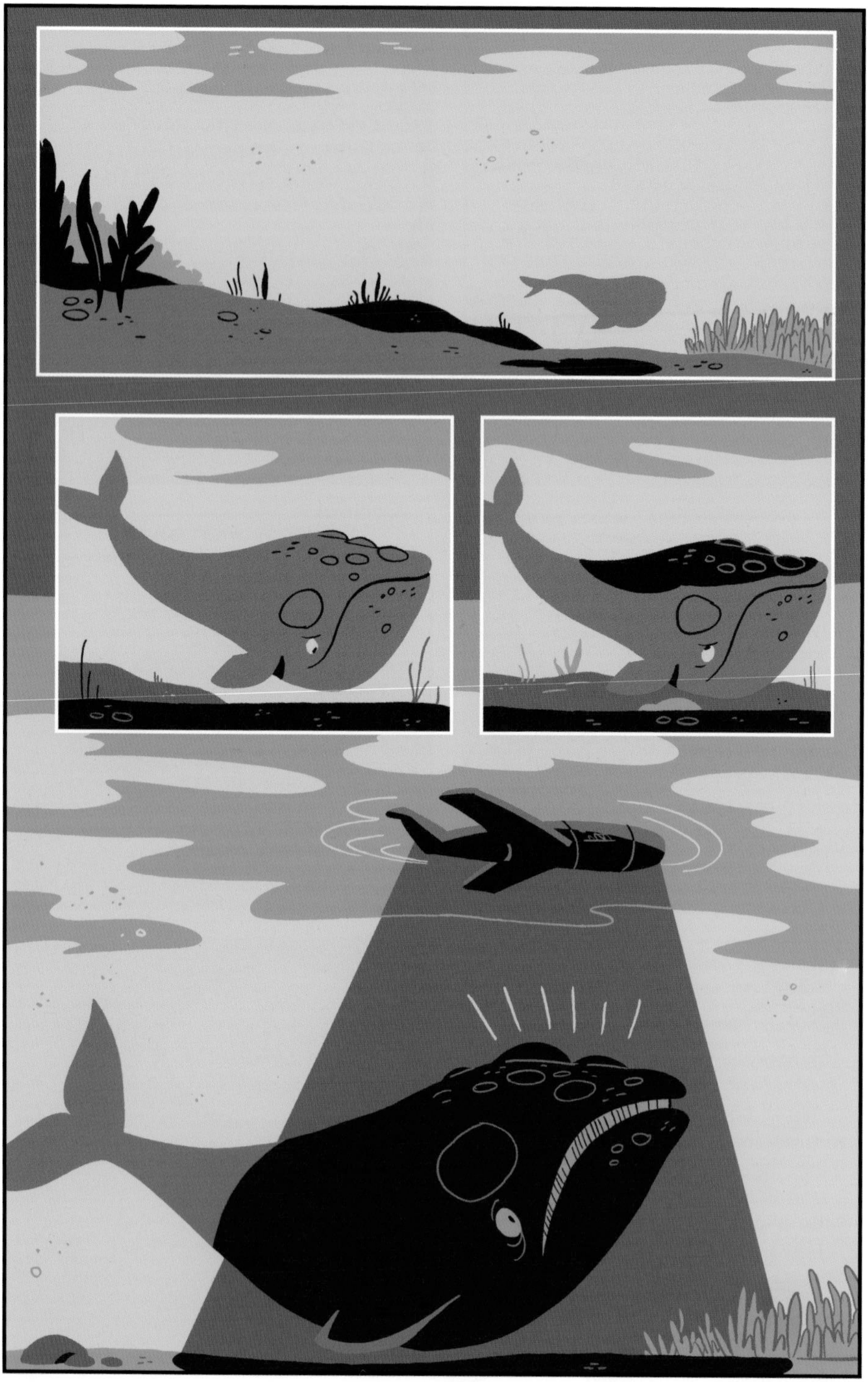

They can send ships down here, too? I wonder what for...

I think they wanted to see how we were using the *FEEDING* grounds.

I mainly eat copepods, a type of *ZOOPLANKTON*: tiny *ANIMALS* that drift with ocean currents.

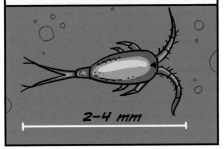

2-4 mm

Other Mysticetes specialize in other zooplankton or small *FISHES*, even squid. Often we get a mix, even if we are shooting for one. The main thing is that we eat a *LOT*.

Krill might be the most important. The whole Antarctic ecosystem relies on them. Down there it's, like, krill heaven *NOW*.

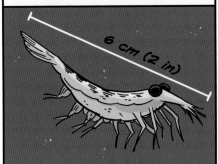

6 cm (2 in)

But how do you even eat these tiny things?

Other baleen whales lunge forward using their loose, *FLEXIBLE* lower jaw and pleats on their throat that they *STRETCH* out, to suck in huge amounts of *PREY.*

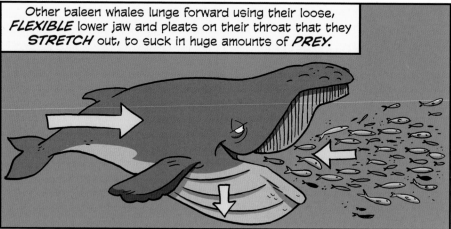

Once our mouths are full, we *PUSH* our tongues up against our baleen. The food gets *STUCK* in the filter, while the water gets pushed *OUT* the sides of our mouths.

Then we just *SCRAPE* the food off our baleen and swallow it. *FILTER*-feeding. *EASY.*

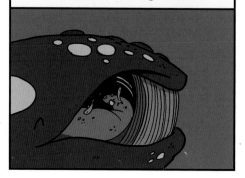

And that's enough to feed whales as big as you and Nova?

We have to eat a *LOT* of them. Like 1,180 kg (2,600 lbs) per *DAY!*

All that *ENERGY* we get from food we use to grow *HUGE*.

A lot of energy goes toward keeping our bodies going and any *ACTIVITY* we do like swimming and feeding.

Young whales like *YOU* have to put energy into *GROWING*.

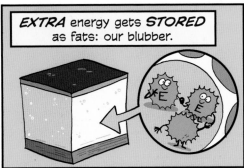

EXTRA energy gets *STORED* as fats: our blubber.

I thought blubber was to keep us warm.

That *TOO*. It also gives us some *BUOYANCY* so we don't sink as fast, but it is mainly *ENERGY STORAGE*.

33

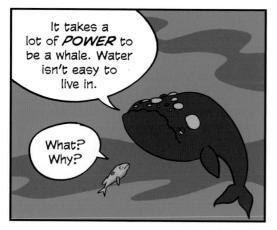

It takes a lot of **POWER** to be a whale. Water isn't easy to live in.

What? Why?

We have to put a lot of **ENERGY** into swimming through it.

Our bodies are streamlined to limit **DRAG**, the force of water pushing **AGAINST** how we want to move.

We use powerful muscles in our **TAILS** to pump our caudal fin, the **FLUKE**, to propel us through the water, while our pectoral and dorsal fins help us turn and balance.

Whoa! Getting food is crazy important, huh?

It is why whales are such good **HUNTERS**.

Like when whales work together to **CORRAL** their prey!

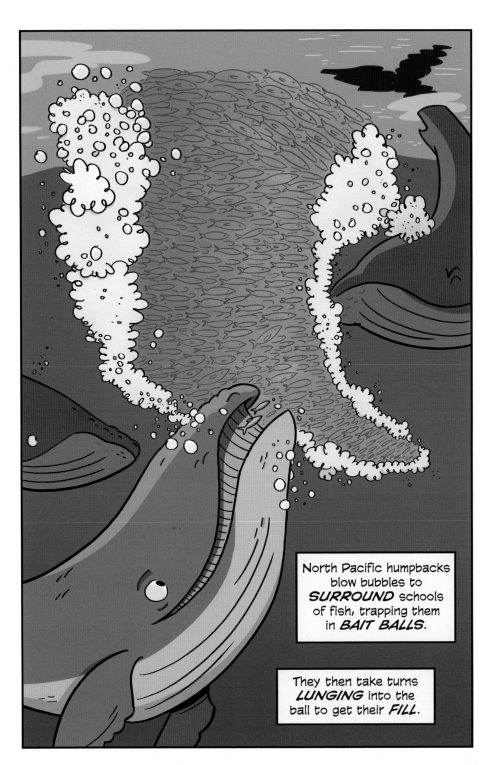

North Pacific humpbacks blow bubbles to **SURROUND** schools of fish, trapping them in **BAIT BALLS**.

They then take turns **LUNGING** into the ball to get their **FILL**.

Whoa... I never really saw us as hunters. I guess I always thought we were more gentle than that.

ALL whales are *CARNIVORES*. We all hunt and eat some kind of *ANIMAL*.

Whether that's Mysticetes filtering *TINY* animals from the water with *BALEEN*...

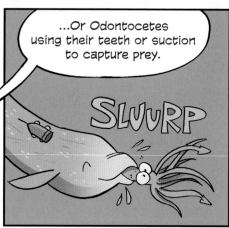

...Or Odontocetes using their teeth or suction to capture prey.

SLUURP

Whales hunt in order to get the *ENERGY* we need to *LIVE*.

Some whales even eat *OTHER* whales.

SPITOo!

What?!

36

Yeah, *THOSE* whales do.

Whoa. We should talk to them!

R-right?

Uh... *OKAY.* Yeah!

Hi! I'm Zip! I'm, um, interviewing whales f-for a podcast—

GREETINGS, O g-great orca! I am Lane, I d-do *NOT* taste good.

Hello, young ones. Call me Inu. I am the matriarch of this pod.

Inu
Killer Whale/Orca
(*Orcinus orca*)

Hey.

Sup?

Yo.

Uh, is—is it true that you eat other whales?

Some of our kind does.

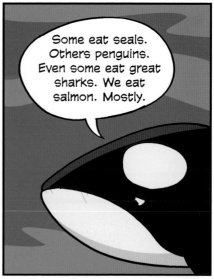

Some eat seals. Others penguins. Even some eat great sharks. We eat salmon. Mostly.

My kind is the *top predator* in our *food web*. We eat salmon, which eat smaller fish, which eat smaller fish and invertebrates, which eat zooplankton, which eat plants, like algae and microscopic phytoplankton.

What's a food web?

Relationships, links, between eaters and eaten. All those found within an ecosystem.

So I'm a part of a food web, too?

A different one. Different whales eat different things. Most are top predators, still.

Or sharks!

Or us!

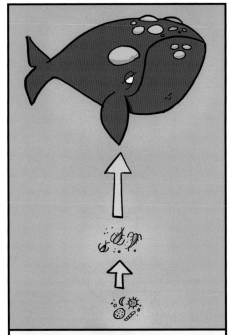

Mysticetes, like your friend, have few links in the chain between top predator and *producers*, those that make food from energy: the phytoplankton and algae for us.

Odontocetes will often have more links in the chain. Orcas to the south of us belong to this food chain. Here, *consumers*, those that get energy from food, eat other consumers until eventually we get to the animals that eat the producers.

Top predators play a critical role in maintaining balance in ecosystems. It is our responsibility to keep other consumers in check, but also not overdo it and wipe them out.

Some organisms in an ecosystem are *keystones*, they ensure the system can exist.

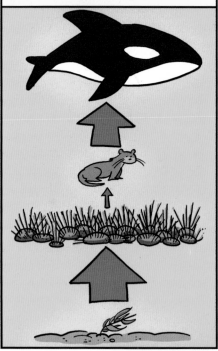

If these keystone organisms are lost, the ecosystem can rapidly fall apart.

Humans are particularly good at this—

Wait!

You've made contact with humans?!

They were tracking your pod with that animal? The dog? Why?

They were collecting our scat and—

Scat?

POOP!

Why would they want your poop?!

Not just that! They were after *eDNA*.

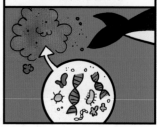

eDNA, environmental DNA, is collected from the water. From scat, yes, but also from skin, oils, and mucus. From the pieces of ourselves we leave behind.

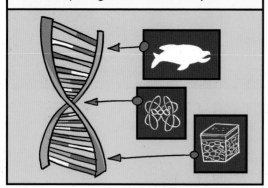

DNA, deoxyribonucleic acid, is one of the building blocks of life. It contains all the blueprints on how to build you and everything that maintains you.

Whoa. It contains the answers to life?

The universe?

Everything?

No! Not all that. Your DNA forms the foundation of who you are. The rest is formed by your environment and your choices within it.

Our DNA reveals our connectivity: who we are related to and how.

Our pods. Our families.

But yes, the humans were after our poop. Feces contain much information as well.

GIGGLE SNKR HAH

What does our poop contain?

SNRK

Nutrients, for one thing. Fertilizer for the plants, the producers, which sustain our food web.

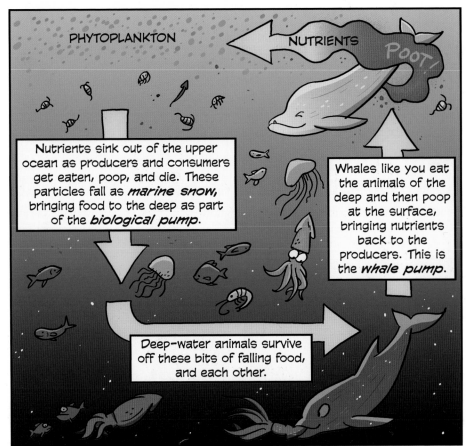

PHYTOPLANKTON

NUTRIENTS

POOT!

Nutrients sink out of the upper ocean as producers and consumers get eaten, poop, and die. These particles fall as *marine snow,* bringing food to the deep as part of the *biological pump.*

Whales like you eat the animals of the deep and then poop at the surface, bringing nutrients back to the producers. This is the *whale pump.*

Deep-water animals survive off these bits of falling food, and each other.

Poop contains more than nutrients.

Information, right? What kinds?!

Undigested bits tell you about diet—what an animal eats.

There are also microorganisms that make up our gut microbiome: the community of tiny, single-celled organisms living within us that help us digest our food and keep us healthy.

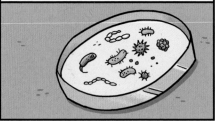

You can learn about someone's health. Different hormones and proteins are made when we are healthy, stressed, or sick.

Poop contains anything bad we've eaten. Toxins.

Pollution

Toxic Chemicals

A weakened whale may not have the strength to swim. They might get stranded on the shore.

There are other reasons this happens, too.

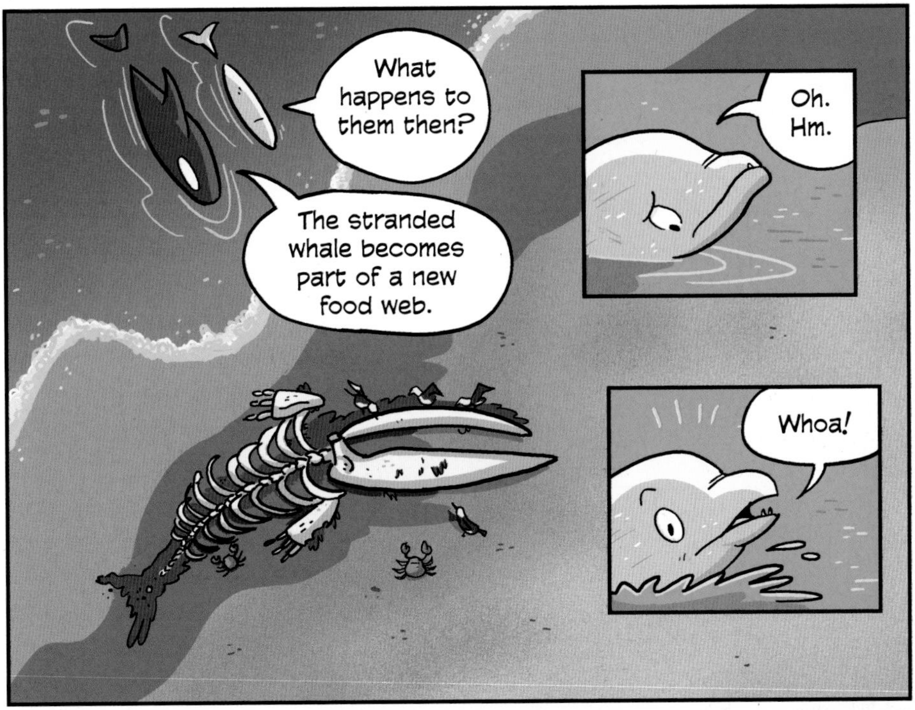
What happens to them then?
The stranded whale becomes part of a new food web.
Oh. Hm.
Whoa!

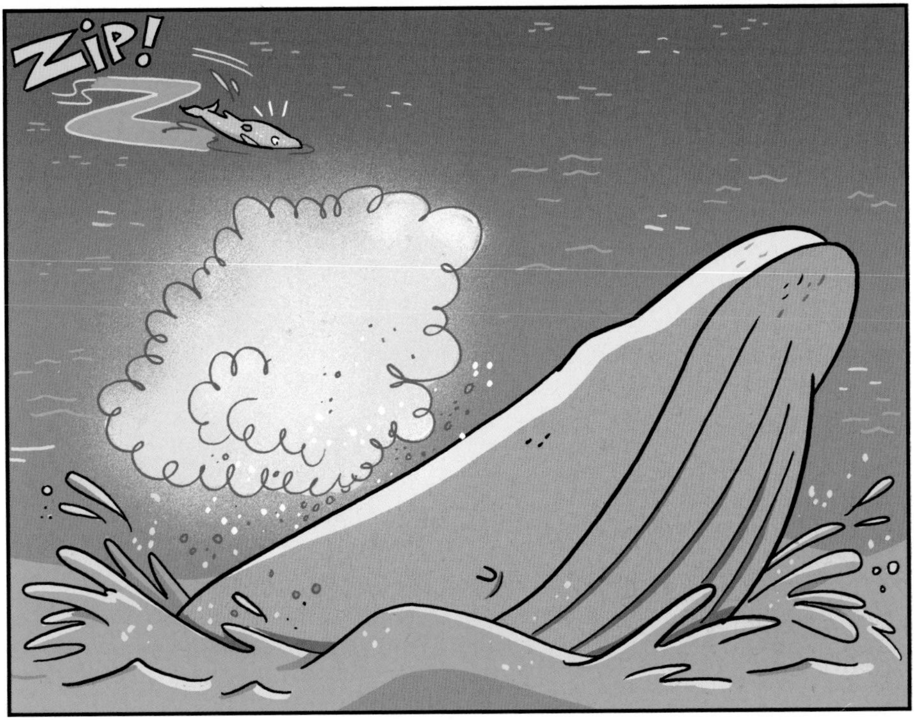
ZIP!

How's it goin', little beaked whale?

Tera
Blue Whale
(*Balaenoptera musculus*)

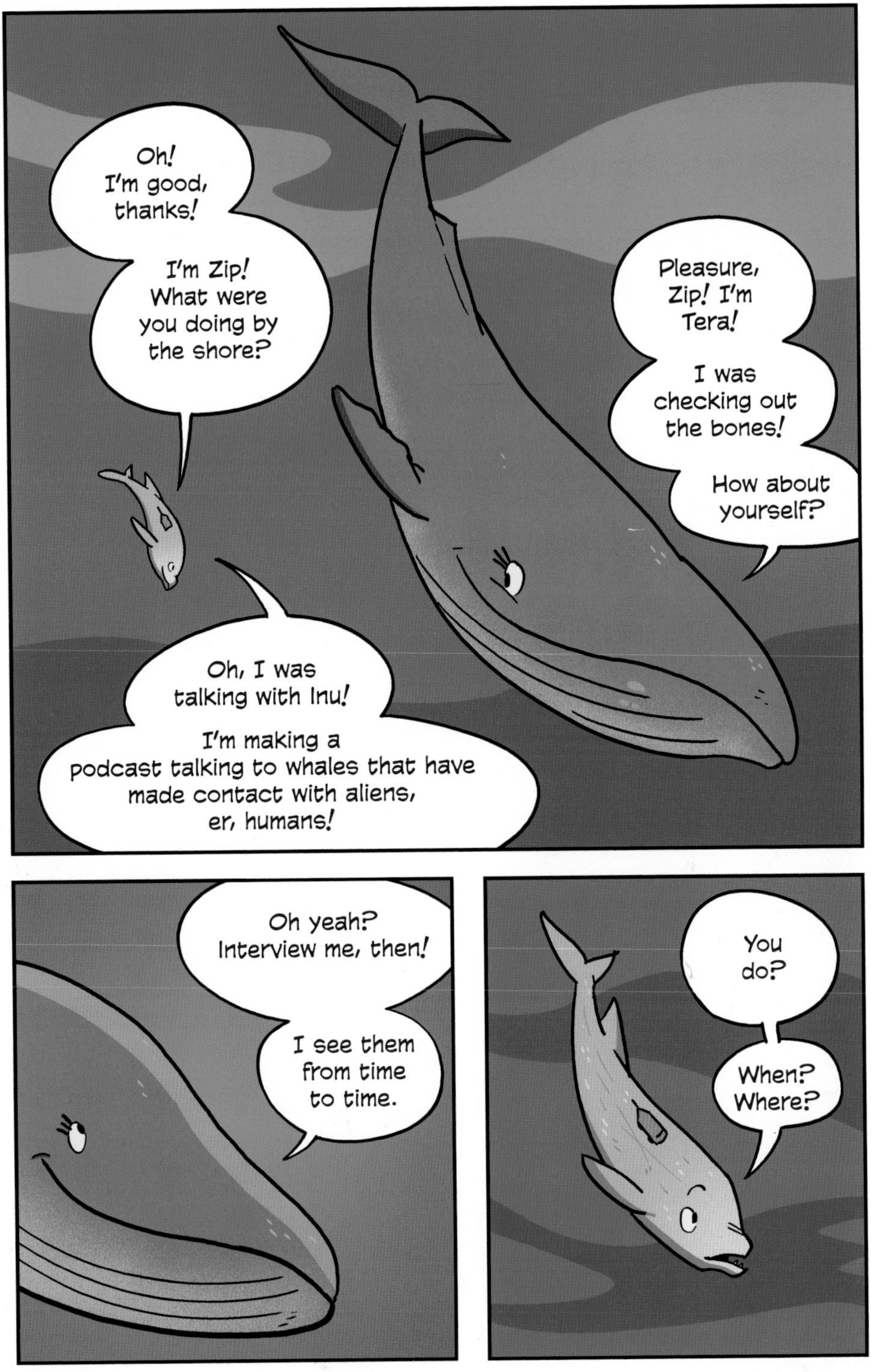
Oh! I'm good, thanks!
I'm Zip! What were you doing by the shore?
Pleasure, Zip! I'm Tera!
I was checking out the bones!
How about yourself?
Oh, I was talking with Inu!
I'm making a podcast talking to whales that have made contact with aliens, er, humans!
Oh yeah? Interview me, then!
I see them from time to time.
You do?
When? Where?

You mean I could've seen them if I stayed by that stranded whale?

Eventually, maybe, yeah.

Huh...

So why are you and them so interested in bones, anyway?

Because bones hold the secrets to how we got to be whales! How we got to be *so big!* How blue whales got to be the largest animals ever to live on Earth (as much as 27 m / 90 ft long)!

Like other vertebrates, animals with a calcified backbone, our skeleton is a framework to support our organs and muscles.

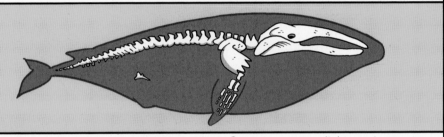

But unlike other vertebrates, a lot of our bones are light and spongy.

Spongy? Like, soft and full of holes?

It is still pretty stiff stuff, but full of holes, yeah.

Bones that support heavy loads are mostly made of dense, compact *cortical bone*. They have to be strong.

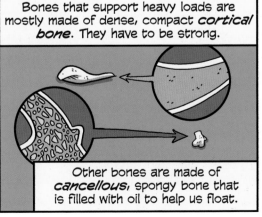

Other bones are made of *cancellous*, spongy bone that is filled with oil to help us float.

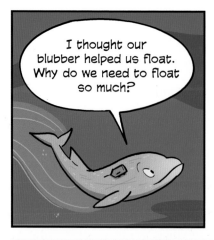

I thought our blubber helped us float. Why do we need to float so much?

Whales are massive and our organs are heavy! My heart alone weighs 180 kg (400 lb)!

An adult blue whale can weigh as much as 173,000 kg (380,000 lb)! That's a lot of gravity pulling us down.

In air, our bodies would collapse under all that weight, but water helps support us.

GRAVITY

WATER PRESSURE

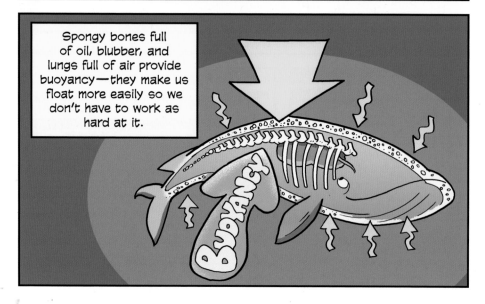

Spongy bones full of oil, blubber, and lungs full of air provide buoyancy—they make us float more easily so we don't have to work as hard at it.

BUOYANCY

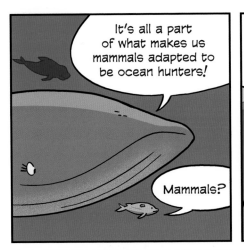

It's all a part of what makes us mammals adapted to be ocean hunters!

Mammals?

Yes! Even though we look kind of fishy, whales are mammals! We have all the classic mammal traits, just adapted for life in the ocean!

Like what?

We get oxygen by breathing air into our lungs. No gills on us!

FWOO

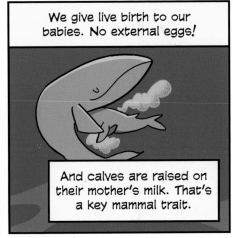

We give live birth to our babies. No external eggs!

And calves are raised on their mother's milk. That's a key mammal trait.

FWOOSH

Okay, so by "traits" you mean features that unite us as a group and separate us from other animals, but what did you mean by "adapted"?

Adaptations are changes to traits that help us survive better in our environment!

Our bodies are shaped from earlier forms in our evolution built for different environments. Related animals often have different versions of the same body parts.

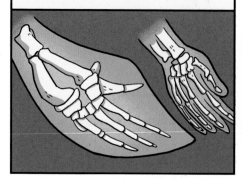

Do we ever lose traits?

Sometimes. Hair is a key mammal trait, but we only have a little or lose it while growing up.

Some whales still have leg bones inside them. They may be vestigial or they may have evolved to serve a new purpose.

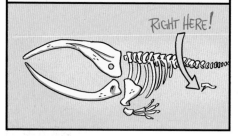

RIGHT HERE!

SLURP

Really? What for?

No one's really sure, yet...

...But they certainly aren't used for walking around on land like our ancestors did!

Whales used to *what?* On land?!

PBBLT

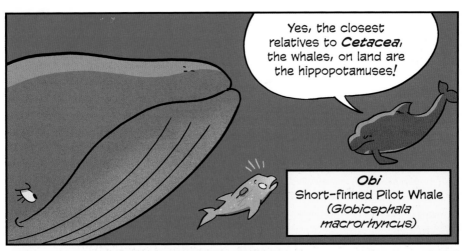

Yes, the closest relatives to *Cetacea*, the whales, on land are the hippopotamuses!

Obi
Short-finned Pilot Whale
(*Globicephala macrorhyncus*)

Obi. Good to see you.

Tera. Likewise.

I'm Zip! Hi! Do we know that from bones?

In part, yes—

But it wasn't clear until we had DNA evidence.

What about manatees, seals, and walruses? They're mammals, too, right?

BREATHES AIR

HAS HAIR

MILK???

Shouldn't they be our closest relatives?

They are mammals, yes! But they share a much more distant ancestor to us than hippos, deer, and other land mammals of the *Artiodactyla*—hoofed mammals with even toes.

Sirenia

Artiodactyla

Carnivora

Seals and walruses are part of the *Carnivora*, a group of meat-eating specialists. Manatees are part of the *Sirenia*, plant eaters. All marine mammals, but the result of taking different paths back to the ocean!

It's a case of *convergent evolution*: when animals of different evolutionary lines develop similar adaptations. Similar environments have similar pressures and different animals can be pushed to develop the same strategies to survive.

SWIMMING WITH TAILS

STREAMLINED

KEEPING WARM

BLUBBER

Evolution refers to changes in traits over time—

That come from changes in DNA that are passed from parents to kids.

But we know about our evolution from the fossil record, which are mostly preserved *bones*.

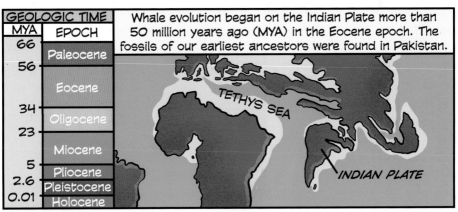

GEOLOGIC TIME	
MYA	EPOCH
66	Paleocene
56	Eocene
34	Oligocene
23	Miocene
5	Pliocene
2.6	Pleistocene
0.01	Holocene

Whale evolution began on the Indian Plate more than 50 million years ago (MYA) in the Eocene epoch. The fossils of our earliest ancestors were found in Pakistan.

TETHYS SEA

INDIAN PLATE

Pakistan? How'd you find out about all this?

Blue whales are good long-distance callers. We make low-frequency, high-energy sounds that can be heard more than 800 km (500 miles) away!

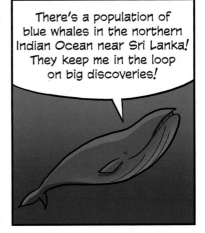

There's a population of blue whales in the northern Indian Ocean near Sri Lanka! They keep me in the loop on big discoveries!

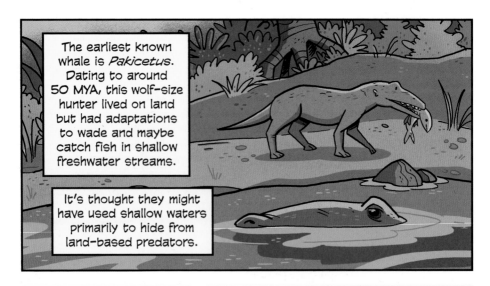

The earliest known whale is *Pakicetus*. Dating to around 50 MYA, this wolf-size hunter lived on land but had adaptations to wade and maybe catch fish in shallow freshwater streams.

It's thought they might have used shallow waters primarily to hide from land-based predators.

Pakicetus shares one key trait with modern whales that no other animals have:

...a thickened part of the bone covering the middle ear called the *involucrum*.

We can't be certain what *Pakicetus* used it for, but this structure helps modern whales tell what direction sounds come from in water.

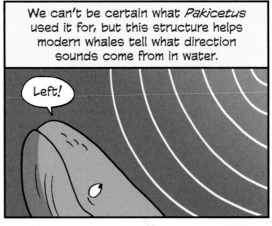

Left!

Wolf?

Like a big dog.

But that's not the only key feature of *Pakicetus!!!*

Their ankle bone, the *astragalus*, was also special! It has a unique double-pulley shape, like two yo-yos stacked on top of each other, which is only found in the Artiodactyla!

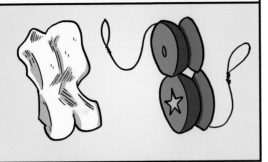

Yo-yo?

CETARTIODACTYLA

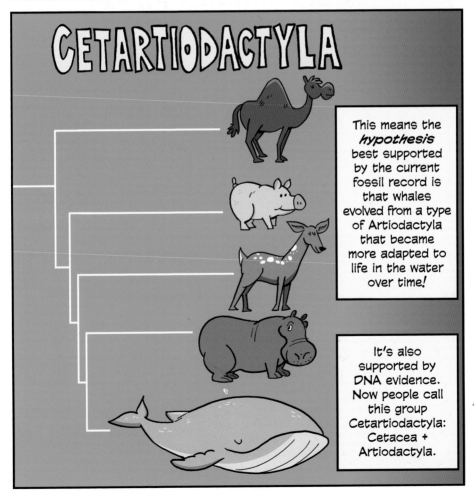

This means the *hypothesis* best supported by the current fossil record is that whales evolved from a type of Artiodactyla that became more adapted to life in the water over time!

It's also supported by DNA evidence. Now people call this group Cetartiodactyla: Cetacea + Artiodactyla.

A nearly complete skeleton of *Ambulocetus natans*, from around 48 MYA, tells us of an ancestor that was living mainly, maybe entirely, in water and had moved to saltier estuaries and coastal waters.

From around 47 MYA, *Maiacetus inuus*, had a flexible spine and may have relied more on its tail to swim. Related fossils are found over a wide range, suggesting that these whales ventured farther into the seas.

Each fossil provides pieces to the puzzle of how we evolved. The lower jaw of *Ambulocetus* had space for fat deposits, which—

Are used by whales to receive sound!

While the *Maiacetus* fossil had a second fossil inside that some think is an unborn fetus, oriented headfirst, which—

Is how land mammals give birth, so it may not have been fully aquatic!

So when did whales become, you know, whale-like?

Whales were way bigger and lived entirely in the ocean toward the end of the Eocene, around 40 MYA.

Fossils of these whales are found in ancient seabeds around the world, like Wadi Al-Hitan, the Valley of the Whales in Egypt.

Two major groups of ancient whales, the *Basilosaurus* and the *Dorudon*, hunted in the warmer waters of the late Eocene ocean, 40–35 MYA.

Saurus?

People mistakenly thought they were reptiles at first.

Crucial shifts in the whale form occurred here! The nostrils moved up and back along the head and the eyes moved to the sides of the head.

The front limbs have become flipper-like and the back limbs are inside, maybe vestigial, but they still have an astragalus!

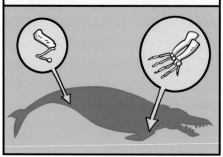

And then eventually they became us! The true whale forms realized!

Nope. That's not how evolution works.

Evolution doesn't have a plan or an end point. It's a constant process of traits being shaped by the environment.

Of survivors passing on their DNA to their children.

Evolution shapes what already exists for new and changing environments. It doesn't decide what will succeed and what will fail.

Fossils at Cerro Ballena, Chile, from the Late Miocene, around 11 MYA, are of large baleen whales, around 8 meters (26 feet) long with pleated, stretchy throats.

Big, but not as big as baleen whales now, because the environment didn't allow or push them to be.

It's only over the last 4.5 million years, across the Pliocene and the Pleistocene, that the conditions became right to become giants.

The oceans changed. There's tons of zooplankton and small fish, but spread out in distant patches, creating the conditions for baleen whales to get...

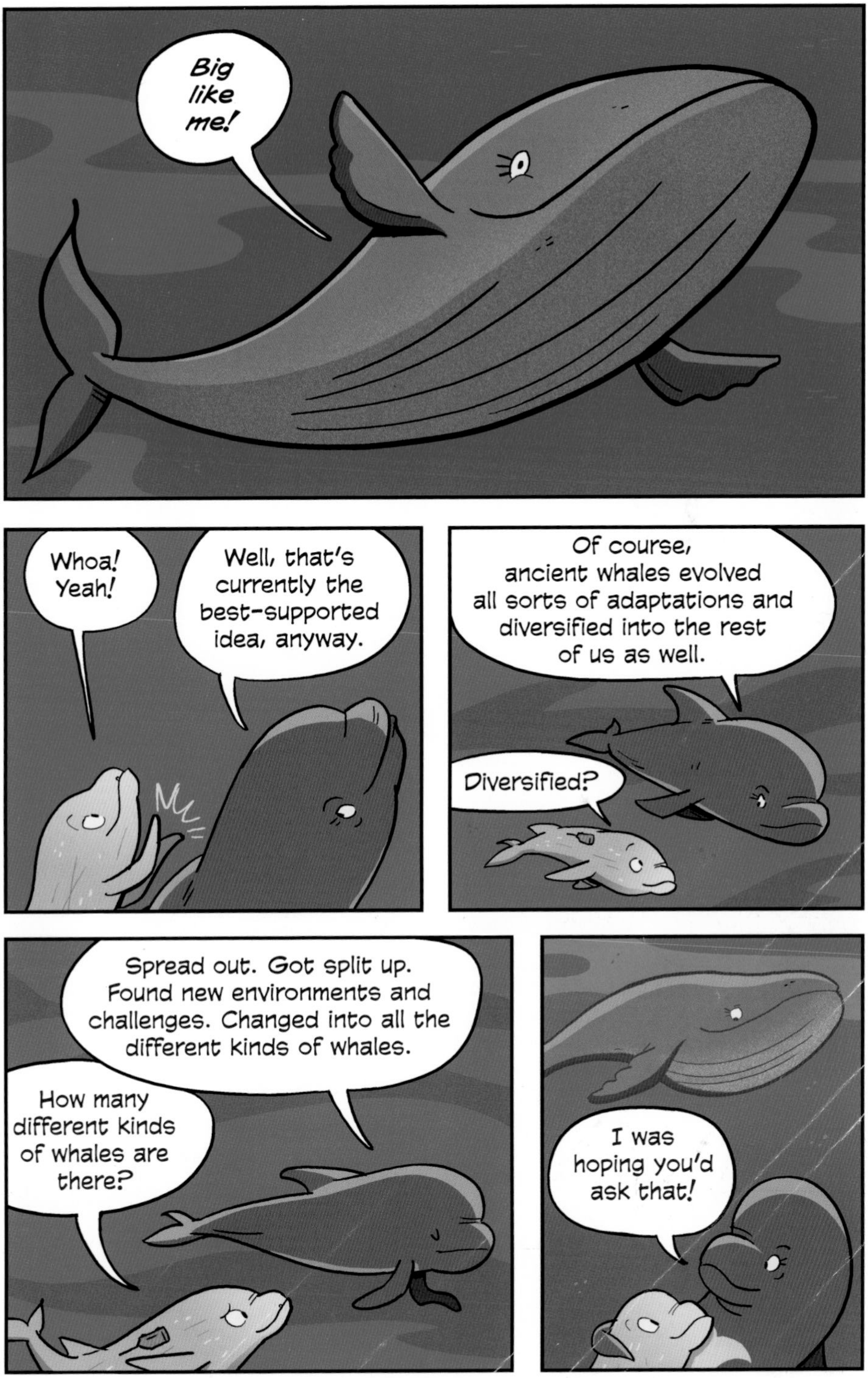
Big like me!
Whoa! Yeah!
Well, that's currently the best-supported idea, anyway.
Of course, ancient whales evolved all sorts of adaptations and diversified into the rest of us as well.
Diversified?
Spread out. Got split up. Found new environments and challenges. Changed into all the different kinds of whales.
How many different kinds of whales are there?
I was hoping you'd ask that!

Zip, do you remember the two main groups within *Cetacea*, the whales?

Yeah! There's the whales that filter-feed with baleen: the *Mysticetes!*

And then toothed whales like us! The *Odontocetes!*

Great job!

Does "cete" mean...whale?

Yes! "Cetus" is Latin for big sea creature. In mythology, it was a kind of big sea monster. The constellation Cetus is named for it and is often called "the Whale."

Latin? Why do you use all these weird words to describe us?

That's *taxonomy!* Putting organisms into groups based on shared traits and DNA. Then giving those groups, and the organisms in them, scientific names!

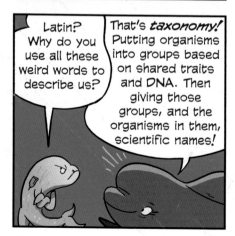

Common names vary between languages and regions, which can get confusing. Take you, for instance. You are a Cuvier's beaked whale but are also called the goose-beaked whale.

Goose-beaked... what's a goose?!

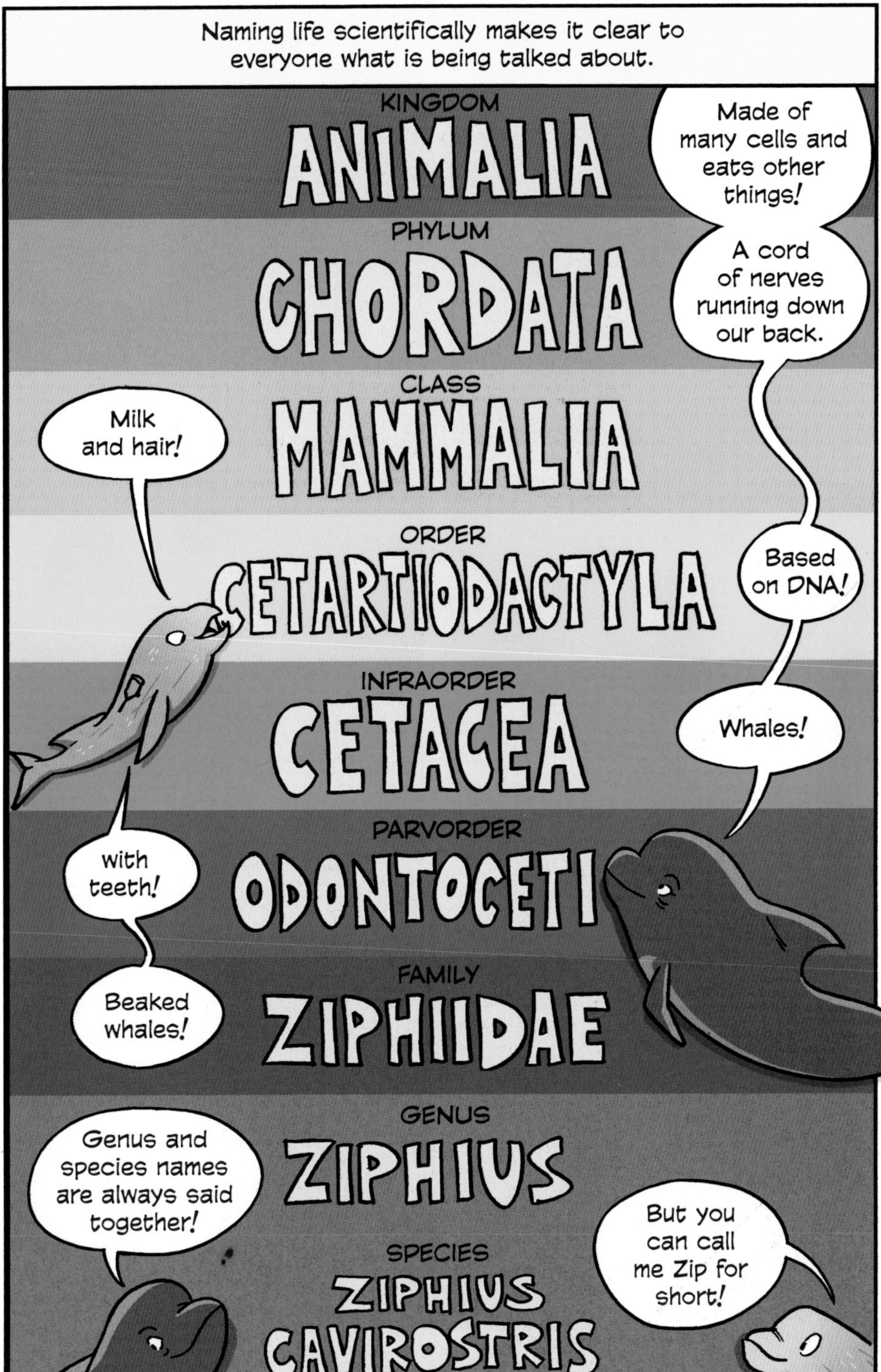

Naming life scientifically makes it clear to everyone what is being talked about.
KINGDOM
ANIMALIA
Made of many cells and eats other things!
PHYLUM
CHORDATA
A cord of nerves running down our back.
CLASS
MAMMALIA
Milk and hair!
ORDER
CETARTIODACTYLA
Based on DNA!
INFRAORDER
CETACEA
Whales!
PARVORDER
ODONTOCETI
with teeth!
FAMILY
ZIPHIIDAE
Beaked whales!
GENUS
ZIPHIUS
Genus and species names are always said together!
SPECIES
ZIPHIUS CAVIROSTRIS
But you can call me Zip for short!

The family level is a really useful way of looking at the *diversity* of whales. Your family is the Ziphiidae (ZI-FIH-ID-EE): the beaked whales!

ALIA
RDATA
MAMMALIA
CETARTIODACTYLA
CETACEA
ODONTOCETI
ZIPHIIDAE
ZIPHIUS
ZIPHIUS CAVIROSTRIS

I honestly don't know very much about them...

Yeah, no one seems to.

So tell me about them, Zip!

Okay!

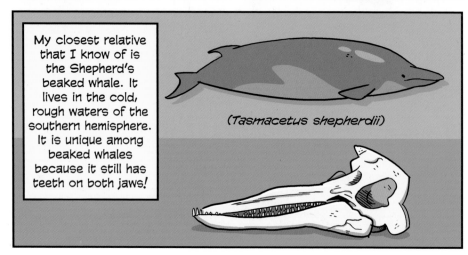

My closest relative that I know of is the Shepherd's beaked whale. It lives in the cold, rough waters of the southern hemisphere. It is unique among beaked whales because it still has teeth on both jaws!

(*Tasmacetus shepherdii*)

Baird's beaked whales are the largest of the beaked whales at around 11 meters (36 ft). They dive down more than 1,000 m (3,281 ft) to hunt fish and squid, and sometimes even invertebrates on the seafloor!

(*Berardius bairdii*)

(*Indopacetus pacificus*)

Longman's beaked whales have bigger pods than most beaked whales, sometimes up to 100 whales! They even pod with other species of whale, like short-finned pilot whales!

Northern bottlenose whales are more curious and active at the surface than most beaked whales. They even sometimes *lobtail*: slap their tail and fluke down onto the surface.

(*Hyperoodon ampullatus*)

SLURRP!

(*Mesoplodon layardii*)

Male strap-toothed whales have big tusk-like teeth that wrap around their mouths, so they can't open all the way! They only need to open it wide enough to suck up small squids!

Gray's beaked whales have a row of tiny teeth in their upper jaws, but they may be vestigial—not really used. They are deep-diving fish and squid eaters.

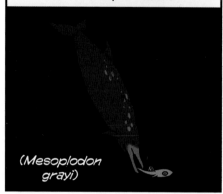

(Mesoplodon grayi)

Blainville's beaked whales don't talk much at the surface—they don't want predators to hear them. They make their sounds while diving for deep-sea squid and fish.

(Mesoplodon densirostris)

True's beaked whales are good divers, too. They have pockets on their bodies to tuck in their *pectoral fins* when diving down to hunt squid and fish.

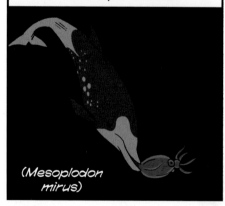

(Mesoplodon mirus)

Spade-toothed whales I've never seen, but have heard about. They are super rare. I guess they dive a lot, probably hunting deep-sea squids and fish?

(Mesoplodon traversii)

It sounds like all we know about most beaked whales is that they probably dive to eat deep-sea squid and fish.

Pretty much, yeah.

There are a bunch of other beaked whales, but I don't know much more about them than the diving-for-squid thing.

There might be more beaked whales I don't know about. I haven't seen them all.

No one has! At least we aren't sure yet.

What family are you from, Obi?

Delphinidae (DEL-FIN-ID-EE)! The oceanic dolphins!

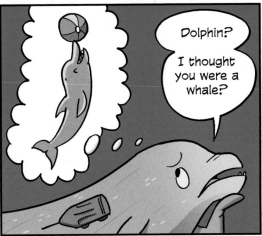

Dolphin?

I thought you were a whale?

Dolphins are whales! Odontocetes like you! "Whale" just kind of means the bigger ones.

Told you common names are confusing.

How'd you learn about all of this?

You haven't guessed yet? I was inspired to learn after I first made contact with humans, just like you!

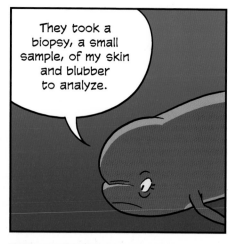

They took a biopsy, a small sample, of my skin and blubber to analyze.

Did it hurt?

No, barely felt it. It doesn't go deep enough to hit muscle, and it pops right out.

The dart is sterilized so we won't get an infection. And dolphin skin heals really fast.

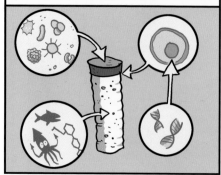

Biopsies provide a ton of information. Blubber can be analyzed for diet and toxins, there's the microbiome on our skin, and, my favorite, the DNA from skin cells!

DNA tells us about who we are and who we are related to, right? Family! Connectivity.

Right! The humans wanted to see if I was from a distinct *population* of pilot whales. Maybe even a *subspecies!*

Too technical?

A bit, yeah.

Right... Sorry.

A *species* is meant to be an organism with distinct traits and/or DNA. Something clearly different. And if it mated with a different species, the *hybrid* wouldn't be able to have offspring.

But many organisms break these rules. Life doesn't really draw lines or make clear categories, and it is always changing. Life exists on a spectrum.

That seems really complicated and confusing.

Yup! Pretty much.

Life can be pretty complicated sometimes. We just have to sort it out the best we can.

Hm... okay. I'll try.

A *population* is a bunch of one species living in a particular place.

If a population is separated from others for a long time, it can become genetically distinct, have different DNA, even if they look the same on the outside.

Each population's DNA is changing because of its unique environment, but those changes aren't shared across the whole species because the groups are so distant.

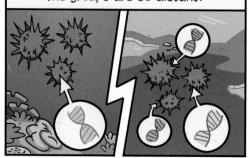

If the same species lives in different environments but has different DNA and body forms to suit those habitats, those different versions of the species are called *ecotypes*.

Orcas are super widespread in the ocean and have a bunch of ecotypes.

They aren't all like Inu and her pod?

Inu leads a pod of northern resident orcas. They stay in coastal waters and feed on fish. Salmon, mostly.

Pods of offshore orcas live out in deeper waters hunting large fish. These orcas even hunt sharks, but the sharks' rough skin wears down their teeth.

Antarctic pack ice orcas hunt seals in the sea ice of the Southern Ocean. They make waves that wash the seals off the ice!

If they stay isolated, different ecotypes can become even more different from each other over time.

If a form of a species has a super-different body or has very different DNA from the rest of the species, then it gets split into a *subspecies*.

So are the orcas different ecotypes or subspecies?

We don't know yet! They could even be different species! How cool is that?!

Orcas are members of the Delphinidae with me, by the way. We are part of a special group of oceanic dolphins called the blackfish.

ORCA

LONG-FINNED PILOT WHALE

FALSE KILLER WHALE

MELON-HEADED WHALE

PYGMY KILLER WHALE

SHORT-FINNED PILOT WHALE

Are there other kinds of oceanic dolphins?

Yeah! A lot.

Bottlenose dolphins are probably the most famous.

They are known for their big brains, relative to their body size. They are very intelligent and social.

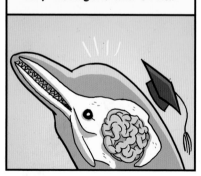

Individual bottlenose dolphins each make their own *signature whistle*, which are used to identify themselves and to find each other in groups, but probably also have other functions.

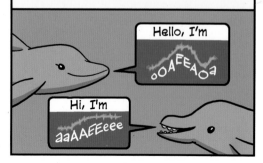

Hello, I'm
oOAFEAOa

Hi, I'm
aaAAEEeee

Spinner dolphins jump and somersault out of the water, but are most famous for their full-body spins, which may be used to knock off parasites. Or it might just be fun!

(Stenella longirostris)

Risso's dolphins are widespread globally, sometimes joining pods of other whales. They usually hunt squid but have been found to eat octopus in the coastal waters of Scotland!

(Grampus griseus)

Irrawaddy dolphins live in the shallow ocean and rivers of Southeast Asia and Northern Australia. They've been seen spitting water to confuse schools of fish they are hunting!

(Orcaella brevirostris)

The Guiana dolphin lives on the Atlantic coast of South America in the brackish waters where rivers and ocean meet. On top of echolocation, it senses the electric fields animals produce to help it hunt prey in the murky water and mud!

(Sotalia guianensis)

Do other dolphins go into fresh water like the Guiana dolphin?

Yeah! The river dolphin families all live and hunt in rivers and estuaries.

South American river dolphins belong to the family Iniidae (IN-IH-ID-EE). The boto hunts for fish, turtles, and crabs along the river and in flooded rain forests.

(Inia geoffrensis)

The Platanistidae (PLAT-AN-IST-ID EE) has just one species: the South Asian river dolphin. Their tiny eyes cannot form images. They may sense light, but mainly rely on echolocation.

(Platanista gangetica)

There used to be another river dolphin family in the Yangtze River in China, the Lipotidae (LI-POT-ID-EE), which had one species, the baiji (BYE-JEE). No one has seen or heard from them in a long time...

(Lipotes vexillifer)

74

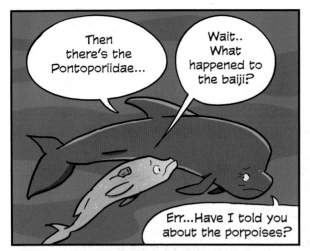

Then there's the Pontoporiidae...

Wait.. What happened to the baiji?

Err...Have I told you about the porpoises?

The what?

Family Phocoenidae (FOE-SEEN-ID-EE), the porpoises!

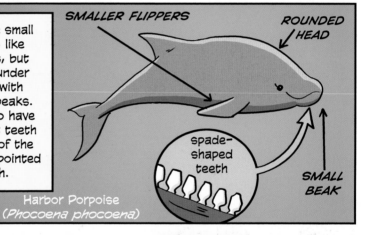

They are small whales, like dolphins, but have rounder heads with smaller beaks. They also have wide, flat teeth instead of the dolphins' pointed teeth.

SMALLER FLIPPERS

ROUNDED HEAD

spade-shaped teeth

SMALL BEAK

Harbor Porpoise
(*Phocoena phocoena*)

Porpoises are small and pretty shy, so they can be rare. The vaquita, (VA-KEE-TAH) is probably the smallest whale there is: only 1.2—1.5 m (4—5 ft) when grown!

(*Phocoena sinus*)

Of course there are like less than 20 of them left now, so...

Huh? What was that?

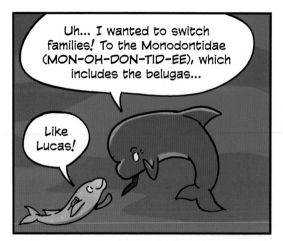

Uh... I wanted to switch families! To the Monodontidae (MON-OH-DON-TID-EE), which includes the belugas...

Like Lucas!

Yup! And the narwhals!

The narwhal's horn is actually a tusk: a big tooth that grows in a spiral out of their head.

It seems to mainly be used to sense their environment.

(*Monodon monoceros*)

But they've also been known to bop fish with them.

BOP!

I can't believe there are whales with weirder teeth than me.

Teeth are what make us Odontocetes after all. Most of us use our teeth to catch prey, like the great hunter of family Physeteridae (FIH-SET-ER-ID-EE), the sperm whale!

Like Mac!

Sperm whales are named for the *spermaceti organ*. A massive organ in their head full of a waxy substance that may help boost and focus their echolocation clicks.

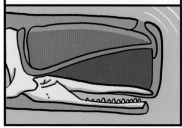

Two possibly related whales, of the family Kogiidae (KO-JIH-ID-EE), also have a spermaceti organ.

The pygmy sperm whale hunts deep-water squids and fishes. They spray a red-brown liquid from a special sac in their intestines when scared to escape predators— like a squid inking!

(Kogia breviceps)

The dwarf sperm whale is a smaller deep-sea squid hunter (we don't know much about these whales). Both of these whales are known for their false gill slit marking that may make predators confuse them for sharks.

(Kogia sima)

That's it for the Odontocetes...

Which leaves the Mysticetes, right? Baleen whales like Nova and Tera!

Right! They are members of the family Balaenopteridae (BA-LEEN-OP-TARE-ID-EE), the *rorquals!*

Fin whales are the second-biggest whale after blue whales. They are known for the mismatched coloration of their head: gray on the left and white on the right (even the baleen)!

(Balaenoptera physalus)

The common minke whale has three subspecies: the North Atlantic, North Pacific, and dwarf forms. The dwarf minke is found in the Southern Ocean where it feeds on small, deep-water lanternfish!

(Balaenoptera acutorostrata)

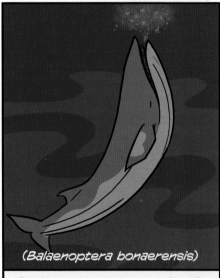

(Balaenoptera bonaerensis)

The Antarctic minke was thought to be the Southern Ocean form of the common minke whale. They look pretty similar, but their DNA divides them as different species!

Bryde's (BROO-DUHS) whale is considered a *complex*, a group of species so similar we haven't yet separated them. The common form is the largest. It is found in warmer ocean waters.

(Balaenoptera brydei)

The Eden's whale is the second species in the Bryde's complex. It is a smaller form that lives mainly in the Indian and Pacific Oceans.

(Balaenoptera edeni)

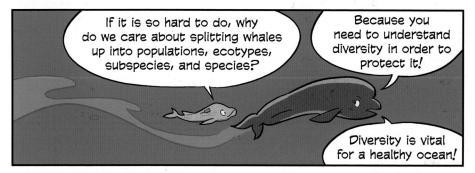

If it is so hard to do, why do we care about splitting whales up into populations, ecotypes, subspecies, and species?

Because you need to understand diversity in order to protect it!

Diversity is vital for a healthy ocean!

Omura's whale was also thought to be an even smaller form of Bryde's whale, found in the tropical Indian and Pacific Oceans, but it is different enough genetically to be a separate species!

(Balaenoptera omurai)

Sei whales look very similar to Bryde's whales, but are known to be a separate species. They have superfine, 0.1 mm (0.004 in) baleen bristles that they use to sieve copepods and other tiny zooplankton from seawater!

(Balaenoptera borealis)

What family was Lane a part of? He's a Mysticete but doesn't look like a rorqual...

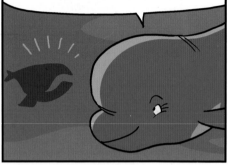

Absolutely right! Lane is a member of the right whales, the Balaenidae (BA-LEE-NID-EE)! They are known for their thicker, rounder bodies and arched mouths.

The three species of right whale, the North Pacific, the North Atlantic, and the Southern, are all known for their *callosities:* rough patches of hardened skin that often get infected by whale lice, barnacles, and worms.

(Eubalaena glacialis)

(Balaena mysticetus)

Bowhead whales live in the frigid waters of the Arctic Ocean. They might have the longest lifespans among not just whales, but all mammals! The oldest known bowhead was estimated to be over 200 years old!

Only two Mysticete families left!

Do we know that for sure?

Probably? Taxonomy changes as we learn more, but some whales are really rare, and the ocean is a *huge* place.

It might never be 100% certain.

The smallest baleen whale, the pygmy right whale is super rare and is actually more closely related to rorquals than right whales. It is the only living species in its family—the Neobalaenidae (NEE-O-BA-LEE-NID-EE)—but the fossil record suggests it might be the last surviving member of an extinct family—the Cetotheriidae (SEE-TOE-THUR-IH-ID-EE).

(Caperea marginata)

The gray whale is also a close relative of the rorquals, but is in its own family—the Eschrichtiidae (ESH-RIK-TIH-ID-EE). They are super well observed because they regularly migrate...

Excuse me, what?

Are you talking to me?

(Eschrichtius robustus)

81

Oh, uh, sorry! We were just talking about different kinds of whales.

For my podcast: *The Zip Files!* I'm Zip, by the way.

I'm Ricky, and this precocious thing is Rob, my calf.

Hey.

Hi!

Anyway, it was nice to meet you, but we have to be on our way. We're traveling north and still have a ways to go.

Oh... I was hoping maybe I could interview you. For the podcast?

Well... I have heard that podcasts are good for road trips....

Okay, you're welcome to tag along.

They watch and record us along our migrations. They try to identify us gray whales by the patterns of our scars, barnacles, and lice, which can be hard since they change.

Humpbacks are more popular. Each has a unique fluke, so the humans can track individual whales making their migration.

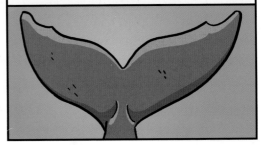

Migration? This big trip you're on?

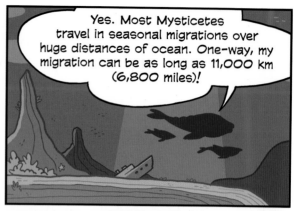

Yes. Most Mysticetes travel in seasonal migrations over huge distances of ocean. One-way, my migration can be as long as 11,000 km (6,800 miles)!

In the spring, we travel toward the pole to eat more than our fill of the prey booming in seasonally warmer polar seas.

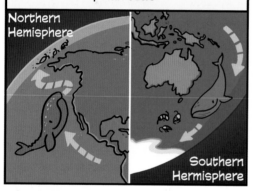

Northern Hemisphere

Southern Hermisphere

Oh! Like Lane! You eat copepods?

No, we gray whales have a special diet.

Gray whales use suction feeding to scoop up mouthfuls of sediment and strain our prey from the grit. We mainly eat amphipods, but all kinds of little animals live in the dirt and we aren't picky.

In the autumn, as it gets cooler, we head back toward the equator to spend our winters in warm, tropical waters.

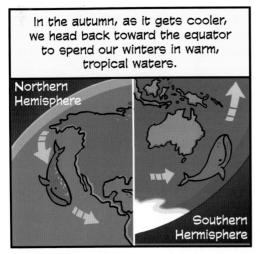

Northern Hemisphere

Southern Hermisphere

And eat different food there?

No, we don't eat during winter or while traveling. We live off the blubber we build up feasting over the summer.

Winter is a time of courtship, breeding, and giving birth.

I just had this one a few months back, but he's big enough to travel now.

Mrrrrm!

Just a second, baby—

Whoa, that's such a huge trip to make every year! How do you know where you are going?

Well, I—

Momma!

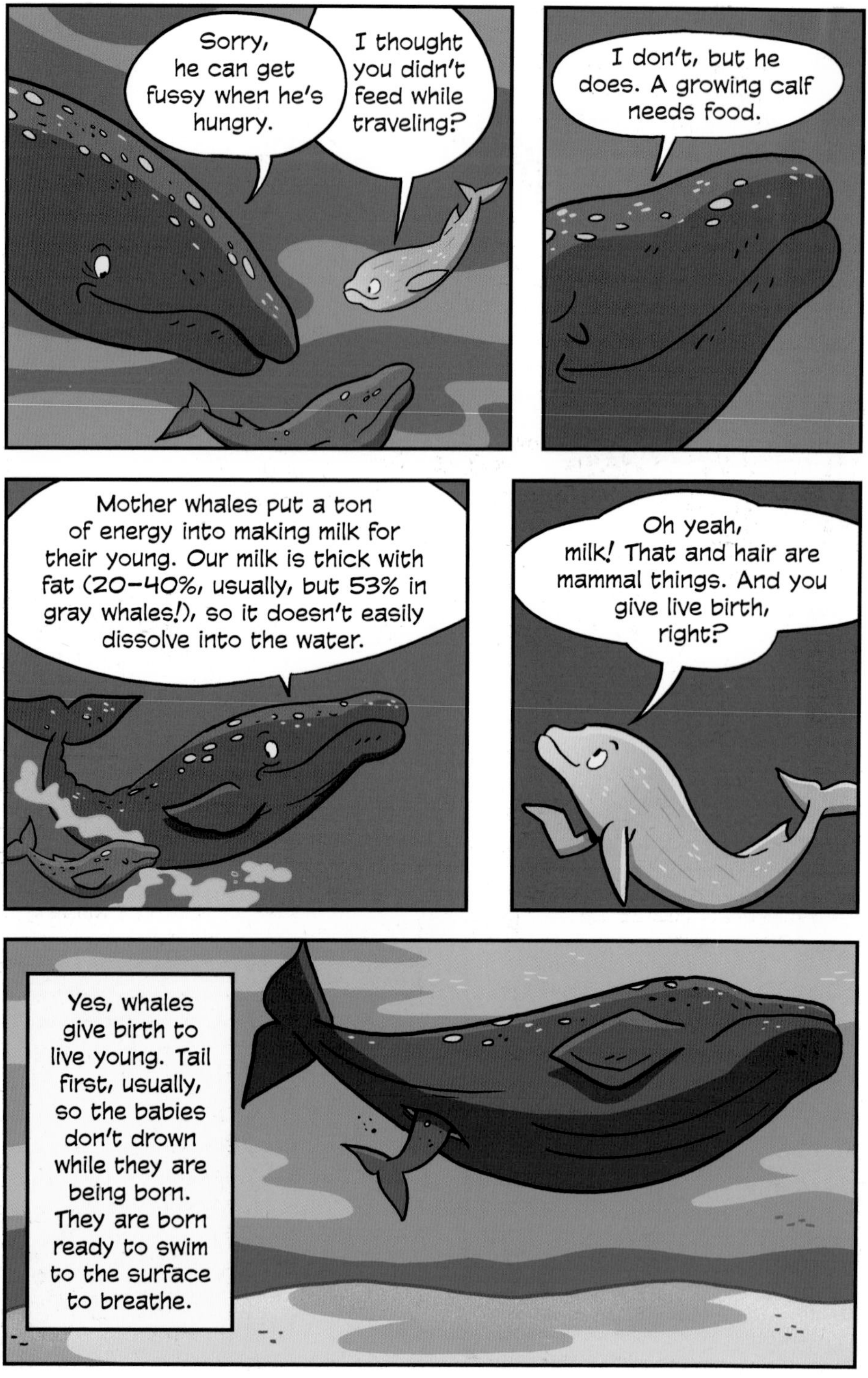
Sorry, he can get fussy when he's hungry.
I thought you didn't feed while traveling?
I don't, but he does. A growing calf needs food.
Mother whales put a ton of energy into making milk for their young. Our milk is thick with fat (20–40%, usually, but 53% in gray whales!), so it doesn't easily dissolve into the water.
Oh yeah, milk! That and hair are mammal things. And you give live birth, right?
Yes, whales give birth to live young. Tail first, usually, so the babies don't drown while they are being born. They are born ready to swim to the surface to breathe.

Of course they need a little nudge from their mother at first.

Aw.

Is that right, little guy?

I can be a little fierce in protecting him, but it can be a dangerous ocean for a little whale.

Protect him from what?

Orcas and sharks, mainly, but other things, too. Your humans, actu—

Grah!

Baleen whale calves grow up fast. Within a year, he'll be an adolescent, off in his own pod, breaking out with lice and barnacles like his mom.

Oh yeah, I was wondering about those, if that's okay with you to talk about.

Thank you for your concern, but being host to all these little creatures is just a normal part of being a whale. A bigger, slower whale, anyway.

Cyamids, commonly called whale lice, live on our skin. They use their hooked legs to attach to wounds, scars, and skin folds where they eat dead skin.

MUNCH

NOM NOM

CHOMP CHOMP

Barnacles can also settle and permanently attach themselves to whales. They filter-feed, too, so we basically just take them around to their food.

Do they hurt?

Hard to say, really. They are just kind of there. The cleaning-off-the-dead-skin thing is nice.

Real parasites can be real trouble, though, especially worms. Tapeworms that live in the intestines of sperm whales can grow up to 30 m (100 ft) long!

Blehhh. It's weird to think of things living on and inside us.

Yes, but that's life. A whale is a lot of things to a lot of different creatures.

What do you mean?

We play a lot of different roles. I am a mother to my calf, and also his food source, guardian, and teacher.

Soon, I will be hunter and predator, digging up my tiny prey from the seafloor.

I'm a floating island to these barnacles, lice, and parasites. Home, food source, and transport all wrapped up into one.

We can learn a lot by seeing ourselves how others see us. By understanding the impacts we have on their lives.

So, I am a predator to squid, but maybe prey to sharks or orcas?

Yes. Even in death we play a role. If surface predators don't eat us, our bodies sink and we become our own ecosystem.

Sometimes when a whale dies, its body will sink all the way to the deep sea (deeper than 1,000 m / 3,300 ft). A whale fall is a feast for a place where food usually snows down in tiny bits. For up to two years, larger, mobile scavengers will gather and eat away the flesh.

For up to two years more, worms and other small invertebrates will colonize the body, picking away the blubber and any remaining flesh on the bones or in the soil. The bones remain for decades, the oils inside them slowly being digested by bacteria, which in turn will feed another community of animals.

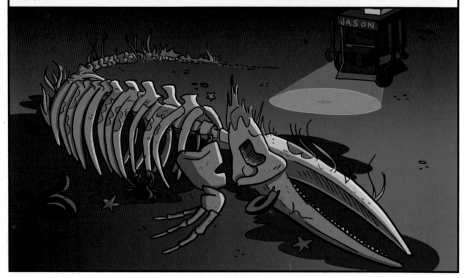

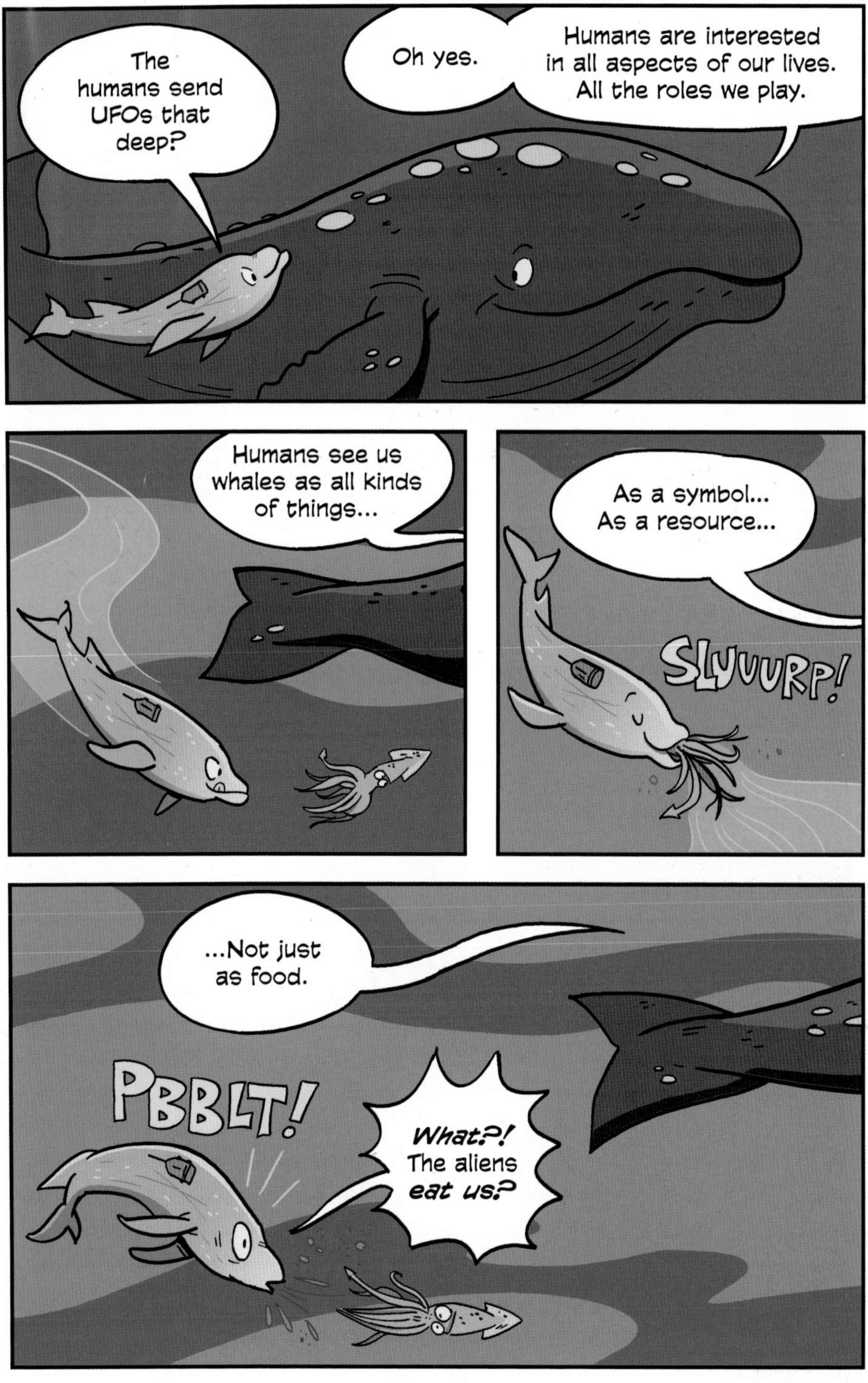
The humans send UFOs that deep?
Oh yes.
Humans are interested in all aspects of our lives. All the roles we play.
Humans see us whales as all kinds of things...
As a symbol... As a resource...
SLYUURP!
...Not just as food.
PBBLT!
What?! The aliens eat us?

Yes, they started out hunting us for food.

The Bangudae petroglyphs in South Korea depict humans using harpoons to hunt whales as early as 6,000 BCE (8,000 years ago).

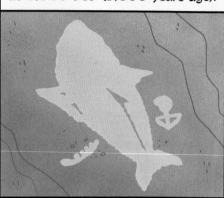

Early whalers attached floats to their prey, slowly exhausting them. Whales provided a huge bounty of food to these peoples.

They ate us in order to survive.

But the humans hunting us changed.

These humans wanted the energy stored in our blubber, *whale oil*, above all else.

Whaling became an industry, with oil as the main product, though they found uses for the other parts of us: bone, baleen, and flesh.

At first they were only able to hunt small, slow whales, but their technology improved. They developed new, more powerful tools to hunt larger whales in more remote and dangerous places.

Factory ships allowed processing to occur at sea, meaning more whales could be hunted on every voyage. By the 1930s, more than 50,000 whales were being killed every year.

The Antarctic blue whale population was brought down from around 239,000 whales to 360. There are believed to be around 3,000 now. About 1%.

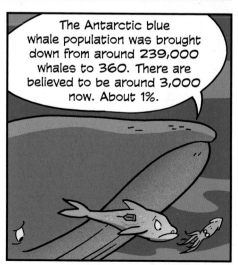

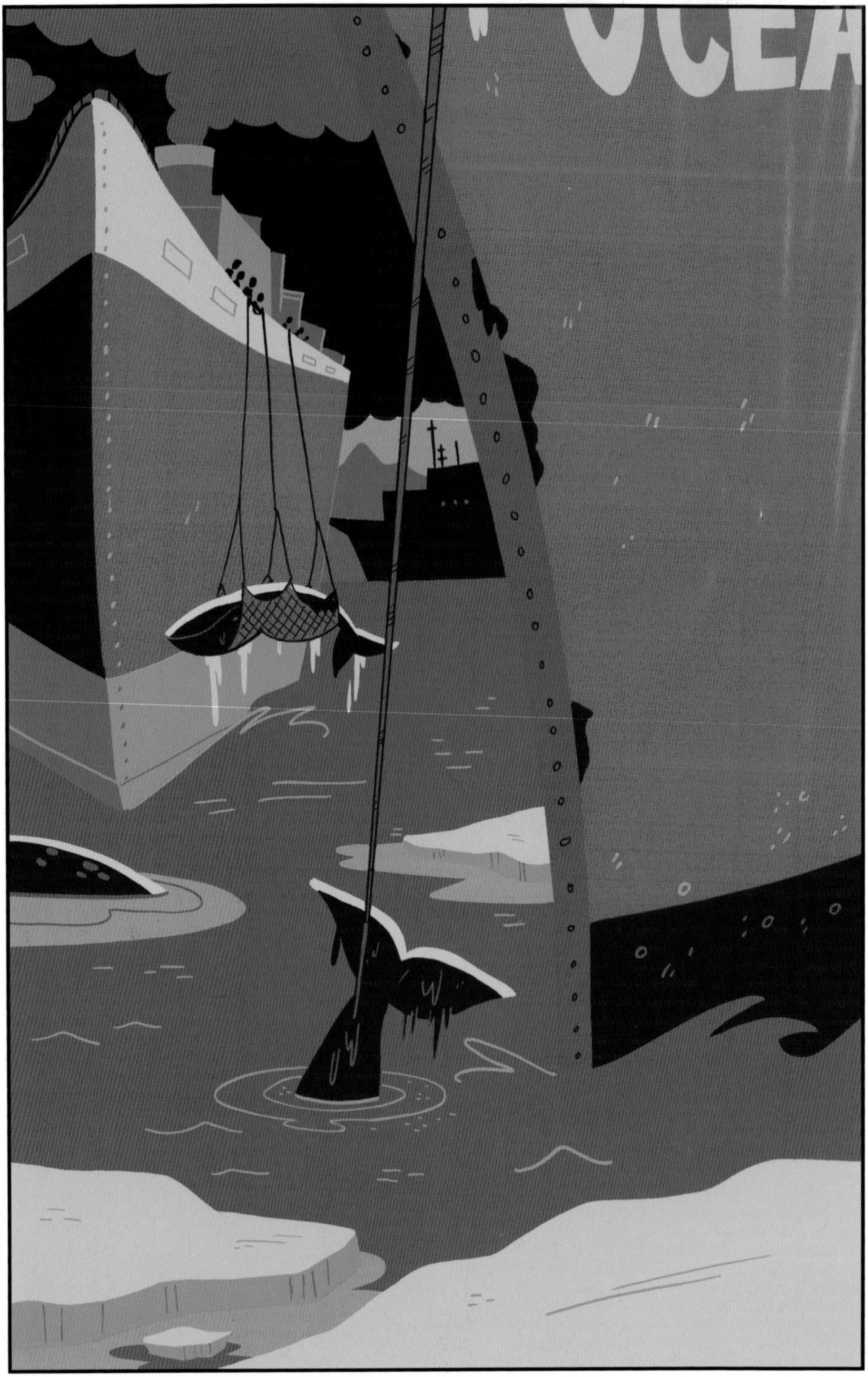
OCEA

I can't believe it. All this time... The humans, the aliens, were...*bad?!*

Really?

What?

You don't really get to say an animal is bad for eating another one. You have tried to eat me like six times now.

Yeah... okay, sorry. But there are a lot of you.

Sure. Eating to survive is fine, but overdoing it is bad.

It's about balance. Taking enough to survive, but not so much that the entire species collapses.

Diversity strengthens communities and ecosystems. Extinction, losing species, weakens them. Ecosystems have to be carefully maintained.

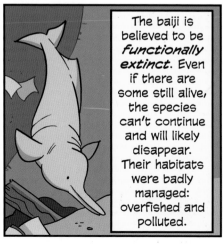

The baiji is believed to be *functionally extinct*. Even if there are some still alive, the species can't continue and will likely disappear. Their habitats were badly managed: overfished and polluted.

They do more than just eat us?! I don't know if I can take this.

They used to respect us. Our world. Some still maintain that tradition...

In *subsistence whaling*, humans take only what they need to live. And to maintain their culture. Their identity. The Iñupiat Community's Nalukataq festival, for example.

Even if they use modern tools, they respect our spirit. They honor what we give to them.

Some, like the Haida Nation, revere us. Respect the blackfish as powerful creatures. Feel our relationship is important. A force of good in the natural world.

They pollute the ocean with their garbage. Plastics break down into *microplastics*. Our food eats these plastics, and we eat prey and plastic both.

Toxic chemicals flow into our waters as well, poisoning our food. Blooms of toxic algae are more common. Our bodies become toxic, with these chemicals stored in our blubber.

A little fish will only have a little toxin. A big fish eats a lot of little fish. We eat a lot of big fish.

The toxins build up as you go up the food web. This is *biomagnification*.

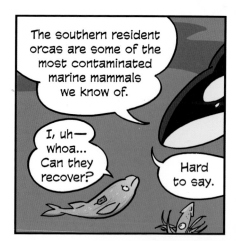

The southern resident orcas are some of the most contaminated marine mammals we know of.

I, uh— whoa... Can they recover?

Hard to say.

Their population had already suffered losses at the hands of humans, who took many into *captivity*.

Where did they take them?

The parks.

The parks.

The parks.

And aquariums.

Because of humans, there is less salmon now. The southern orcas that remain are starving.

Hungry toothed whales will take an easy meal. *Depredation*, stealing from fishing boats, upsets the humans.

So long!

And thanks for all the fish!

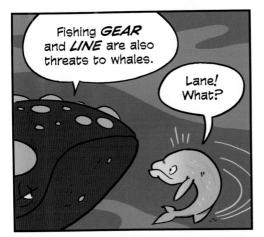

Fishing *GEAR* and *LINE* are also threats to whales.

Lane! What?

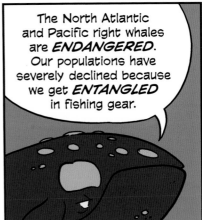

The North Atlantic and Pacific right whales are *ENDANGERED*. Our populations have severely declined because we get *ENTANGLED* in fishing gear.

Fishing line and gear cause *DRAG*, making it harder for a whale to swim. If the gear is buoyant, it can make it harder to *DIVE*, too.

DRAG

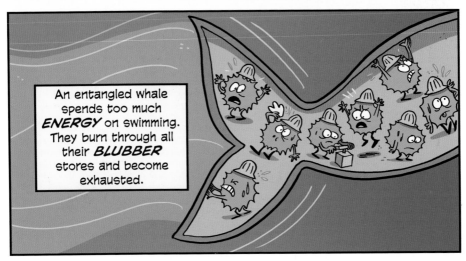

An entangled whale spends too much *ENERGY* on swimming. They burn through all their *BLUBBER* stores and become exhausted.

Without energy, female whales can't make *MILK* to raise *CALVES*. Even if the gear comes off, it can damage our skin and leave *SCARS*.

Oh...

Smaller whales can get tangled in fishing *NETS* or on hooks and be caught by accident, as *BYCATCH*.

Gillnets are designed to capture fish by their gills, but if a whale gets *STUCK* to a net, it won't be able to surface and breathe.

Why don't they just stop fishing?

They rely on fishing to live.

There isn't an easy *SOLUTION*, but things need to *CHANGE*.

The entire *VAQUITA* species is down to less than 20 individuals or so. It is still in *DECLINE*, even though gillnets were banned.

Is this everyone?

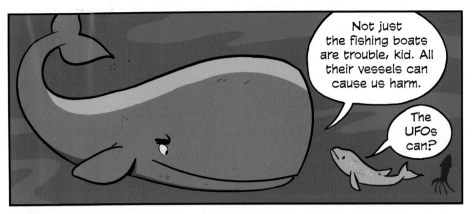

Not just the fishing boats are trouble, kid. All their vessels can cause us harm.

The UFOs can?

We rest and breathe at the surface. Humans driving ships don't always see us, or they go too fast to stop.

A *ship strike* can cause a lot of damage to a whale.

Boats are loud, too!

What?

Some boats use *echosounders* to check depth. Machines that echolocate! But they are loud. And may scare whales.

Some humans use even stronger *sonar*. They use high-energy, mid-frequency sounds to navigate and find other vessels, but it is super loud!

And that's bad?

It is so loud it can not only scare and confuse us, but might cause hearing damage.

If we are scared when we are diving, kid, we might surface too fast and get the bends.

In both cases, we might be so stressed out or hurt that we end up stranding ourselves.

As humans build and use the coasts more, they are making the ocean much noisier.

VRRRRM
BANG
BANG
BANG
BEEP!

A loud ocean makes it harder for us to hear each other. We might be losing our hearing more, too.

And sound is everything to a whale.

That's just one way humans are changing the ocean.

It's a lot warmer than it used to be, and there is less sea ice. Remember?

Yeah...

That's humans, too. Changing the climate by changing the gases in the atmosphere. Increasing carbon dioxide, especially.

Carbon dioxide traps heat energy released by the Earth. More carbon dioxide, more heat trapped, like a denser blanket around the Earth.

CO_2

Whales have adapted to a lot of ocean changes, though, and quickly, too.

Yeah, but nothing this fast.

For animals that grow and reproduce as slowly as whales, the changes are happening so fast that it is going to be hard to keep up.

We don't really know all the ways whales could be affected.

103

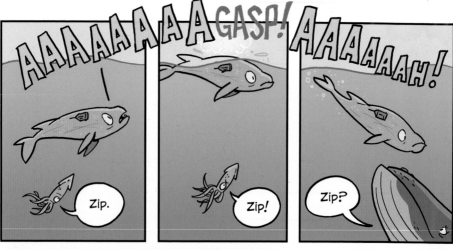

Zip.

Zip!

Zip?

You've made the voyage home! What's the matter, dear?

Humans! Aliens! I don't know. They hunt us. They are making the world worse for whales!

Ah. True enough. But that isn't all that humans do, little one.

Oh no. There's more?!

Many humans also care about whales. Whale-watching boats can be bothersome, but they come because humans are interested in us: in who we are and what we do.

They are probably just trying to figure out which one of us they want to *eat* or make into *oil* next.

It isn't fair to assume they all think that way, Zip.

How you see something depends on the role it plays in your life, your relationship with it. Some humans see whales as a resource, yes, and others revere you.

You're a predator to me, remember?

Many of them simply want to understand us and are taking actions to make things better for whales.

Many humans work very hard to rescue stranded whales. If trained experts can get to a beached whale early enough, they can help us back into the water with minimal harm.

Others go out on their boats to disentangle whales and other sea life caught in fishing gear. This work is dangerous for the humans, but they go because they want to help.

I guess that's cool, but if there are aliens that want to hurt us, or eat us anyway, and aliens that want to help us, who decides what they do?

The ocean is a shared space.

The humans have to come to an agreement. A compromise.

In 1946, the International Whaling Commission was created to *conserve* whales and manage whaling. In 1982, whaling for money was banned worldwide so whale populations could recover.

But not all humans agree with the ban.

Different groups of humans, different cultures and countries, all see their relationship to whales differently. Some feel they could hunt whales *sustainably*, so that we don't die out, but others aren't sure that's true.

That sounds complicated.

It is, dear. They have to decide what they think is right and how to best manage their relationship with us.

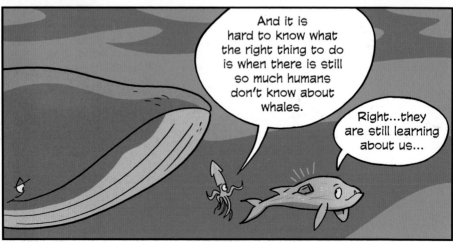

And it is hard to know what the right thing to do is when there is still so much humans don't know about whales.

Right...they are still learning about us...

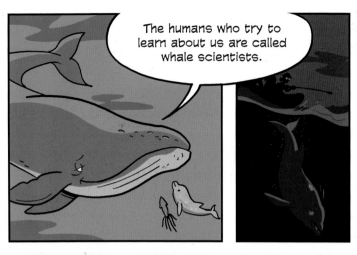

The humans who try to learn about us are called whale scientists.

They use tools to try and answer questions, discover new things about our lives,

RESEARCH

to inform how humans manage their relationship with us. You know them well...

Those ali—the humans I met, that everyone met, were whale scientists?!

Yeah! They were researching whales! And not just gathering data, but stories!

Stories?

Like how you interviewed whales for your podcast, Zip. Sometimes facts and numbers aren't enough. Stories help connect people with information they might find hard to understand or believe.

I want humans to understand us. I want to believe in them. What story should I tell?

Zip, dear. They attached the microphone to you. They want to hear what you have to say.

Your story.

My story...

Okay. Um...

I guess we'll start with what you already know and build from there?

FWOO

GASP

I'm, um, a beaked whale. A mammal. Even though I live in water I breathe air.

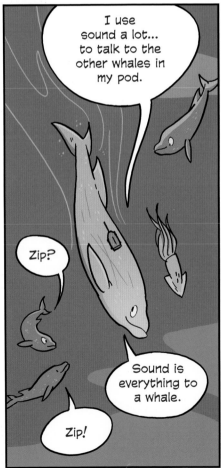

I use sound a lot... to talk to the other whales in my pod.

Zip?

Sound is everything to a whale.

Zip!

I'm a toothed whale, an, um, Odontocete, and use echolocation clicks to find food.

I mostly eat squid (except for one).

I am capable of diving deeper, at least 3,000 m (9842 ft), and for longer (as much as 3½ hours on a single dive) than most other types of whales. But typically I prefer short, shallower dives, like 20 minutes at 300 m (984 ft) or so.

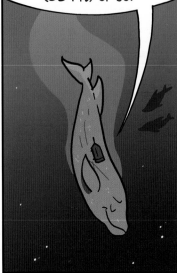

I can hold my breath because I store a lot of oxygen in my muscles and blood.

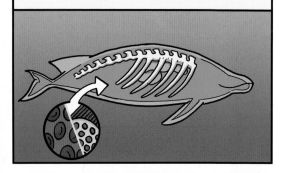

I dive to feed, and then store the energy from food in my blubber, which helps keep me warm.

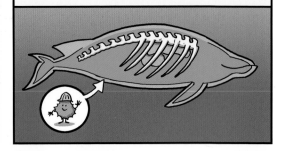

Even though I, um, sort of have teeth, I eat by sucking up food and swallowing it whole.

GULP

Pretty much only male beaked whales get teeth. We maybe use them to fight with each other, sometimes over females, or to try and impress females...

I play a couple roles in my ecosystem. I'm a predator, I hunt squid, but I can also be prey for sharks and, um, orcas.

Cetaceans, whales, evolved from land mammals that adapted to be hunters in the sea in the Eocene (around 50 MYA).

Beaked whales, the family Ziphiidae, evolved in the early Miocene (around 20 MYA) and diversified in the middle Miocene. Fossils are found in Belgium, Peru, and South Africa.

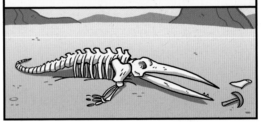

I talked about some of the beaked whales with Obi. I think there are at least 23 species...but the ocean is huge, we dive a lot, and we can live in hard-to-reach places, so I'm not sure.

There are probably more species that I don't even know about.

Maybe you'll find them some-day!

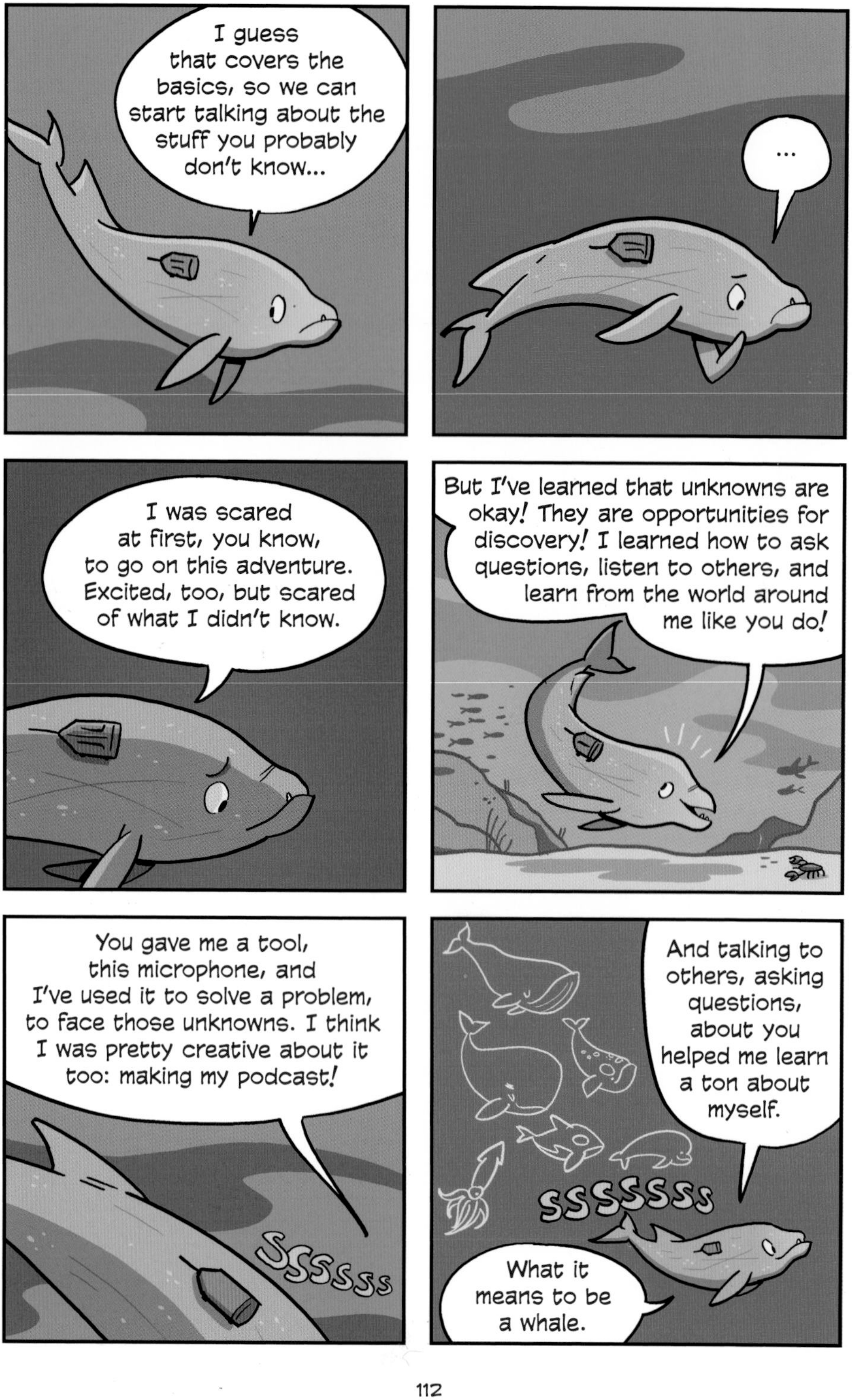
I guess that covers the basics, so we can start talking about the stuff you probably don't know...
...
I was scared at first, you know, to go on this adventure. Excited, too, but scared of what I didn't know.
But I've learned that unknowns are okay! They are opportunities for discovery! I learned how to ask questions, listen to others, and learn from the world around me like you do!
You gave me a tool, this microphone, and I've used it to solve a problem, to face those unknowns. I think I was pretty creative about it too: making my podcast!
SSSSSS
And talking to others, asking questions, about you helped me learn a ton about myself.
SSSSSSSS
What it means to be a whale.

And I think understanding how you see me helps me see how I, how whales, fit into the world. Even if the relationship between humans and whales is...complicated.

SSSSSs

The world is scary and complicated sometimes. I think I kind of, um, alienated you because of that fear.

POP!

But we just have to try and manage our relationship with each other and the world the best we can, right? Keep learning so it's not so scary. So we can make better decisions, right? Huh?

Oh no! Aw...

We had more about beaked whales to talk about!

It's okay, I guess...

They'll figure it out eventually.

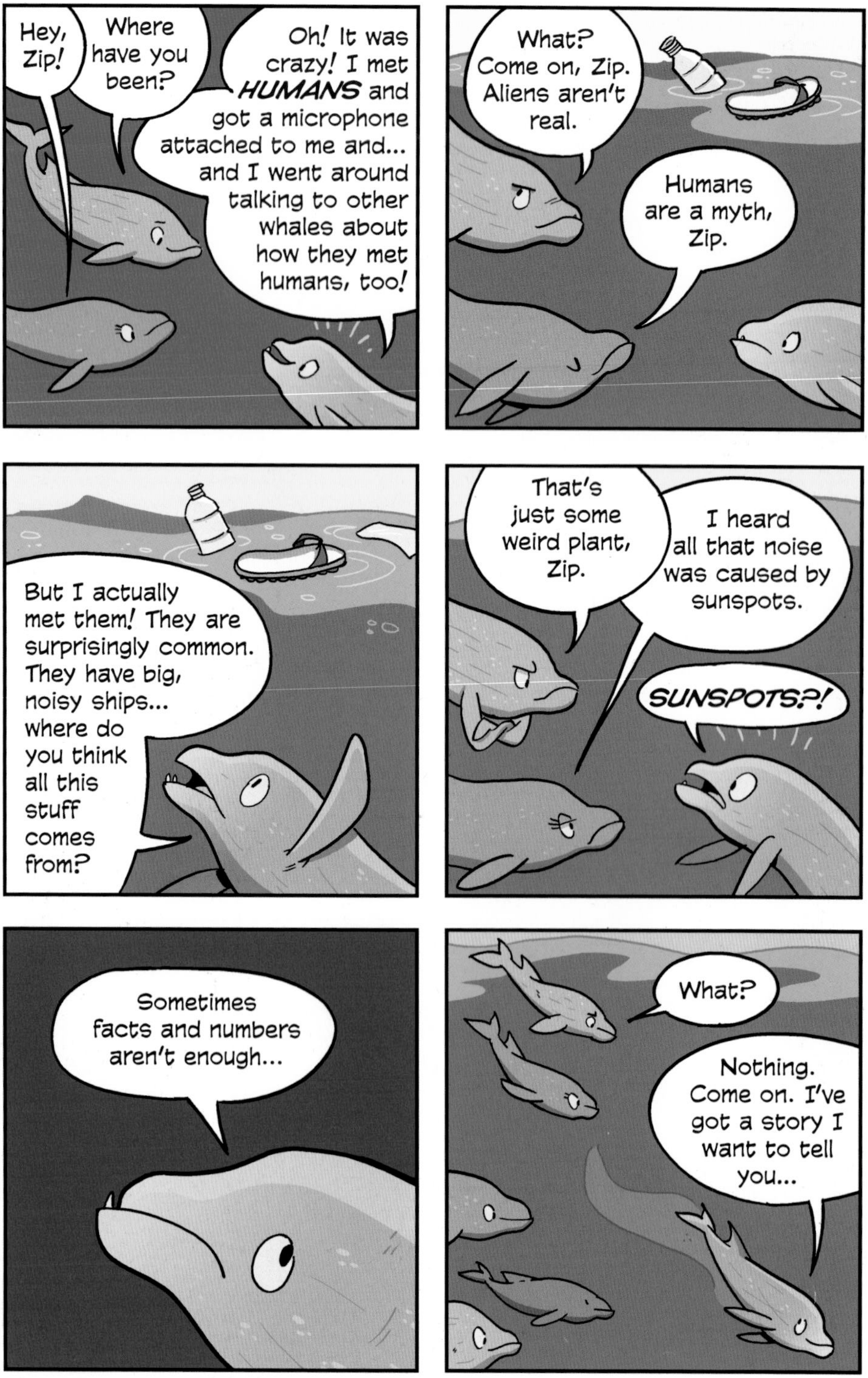
Hey, Zip!
Where have you been?
Oh! It was crazy! I met HUMANS and got a microphone attached to me and... and I went around talking to other whales about how they met humans, too!
What? Come on, Zip. Aliens aren't real.
Humans are a myth, Zip.
But I actually met them! They are surprisingly common. They have big, noisy ships... where do you think all this stuff comes from?
That's just some weird plant, Zip.
I heard all that noise was caused by sunspots.
SUNSPOTS?!
Sometimes facts and numbers aren't enough...
What?
Nothing. Come on. I've got a story I want to tell you...

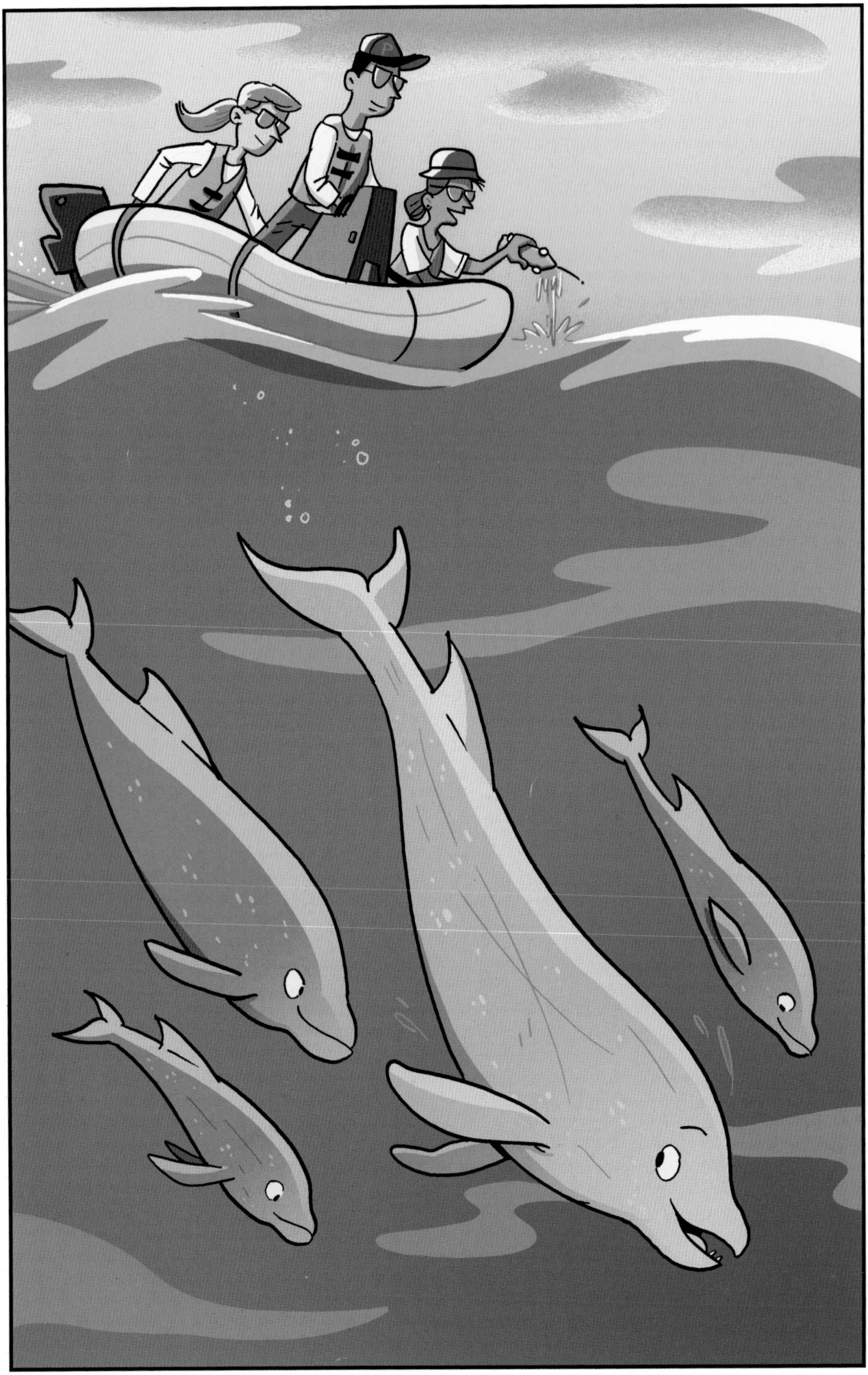

—WHALE GLOSSARY—

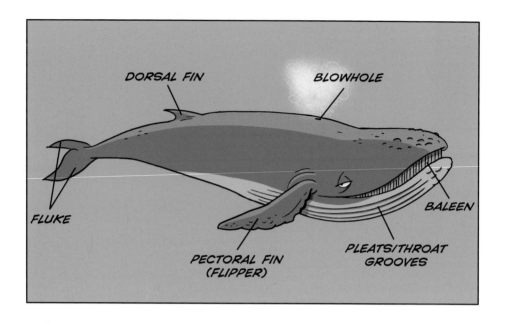

DORSAL FIN

BLOWHOLE

FLUKE

PECTORAL FIN
(FLIPPER)

PLEATS/THROAT
GROOVES

BALEEN

TAXONOMY

Cetacea
The group (infraorder) that includes all whales.

Mysticetes
Baleen whales (of the parvorder Mysteceti).

Odontocetes
Toothed whales (of the parvorder Odontoceti).

BEHAVIORS

Breaching
When a whale leaps out of the water, sometimes completely, and crashes back down onto the surface.

Lobtailing
When a whale, whose body is mostly underwater, slaps its tail down against the water's surface.

VOCALIZATIONS

Clicks
Quick, very-high-frequency sounds used primarily for **echolocation**, but also to communicate.

Pulsed Calls
Higher-frequency sounds made in short, repeated bursts.

Song
A long pattern of sounds produced by some baleen whales, most famously male humpback whales.

Whistles
Higher-frequency sounds made in longer, continuous sweeps of sound. Used for communication and as an identifier (signature whistles) in some species.

—HUMAN IMPACT GLOSSARY—

Biomagnification
The process of substances, like toxins and microplastics, building up as you move up a food chain (e.g., a whale eating a lot of fish containing the substance).

Bycatch
Whales caught unintentionally in fishing nets.

Captivity
Whales removed from the environment to be kept in parks and aquariums are kept in **captivity.**

Climate Change
A change in global or regional climate patterns, in particular a change apparent from the mid to late 20th century onward and attributed largely to the increased levels of atmospheric carbon dioxide produced by the use of fossil fuels.

Depredation
When hungry whales steal fish from fishing lines and nets.

Entanglement
Whales getting caught in the ropes and line used for fishing and other activities, often dragging the line and gear with them and scarring the skin.

Extinction
A species is extinct when it no longer exists alive on the planet. If individuals remain, but not enough for a species to recover, the species is considered **functionally extinct.**

Industrial Whaling
The hunting of whales in order to sell their meat and other products (such as whale oil, historically).

Noise Pollution
Humans producing loud, unnatural sounds that may scare whales, drown out sounds used for navigation and communication, and impair hearing.

Ship Strike
When a ship hits a whale.

HOW TO HELP? GET INVOLVED!
• Learn, share, and discuss!
• Express your ideas creatively!
• Visit aquariums and museums!
• Write letters to politicians!
• Support whale science!
• Fundraise for whale charities!

Talk about whales with your friends and family!

Let's work on solutions together!

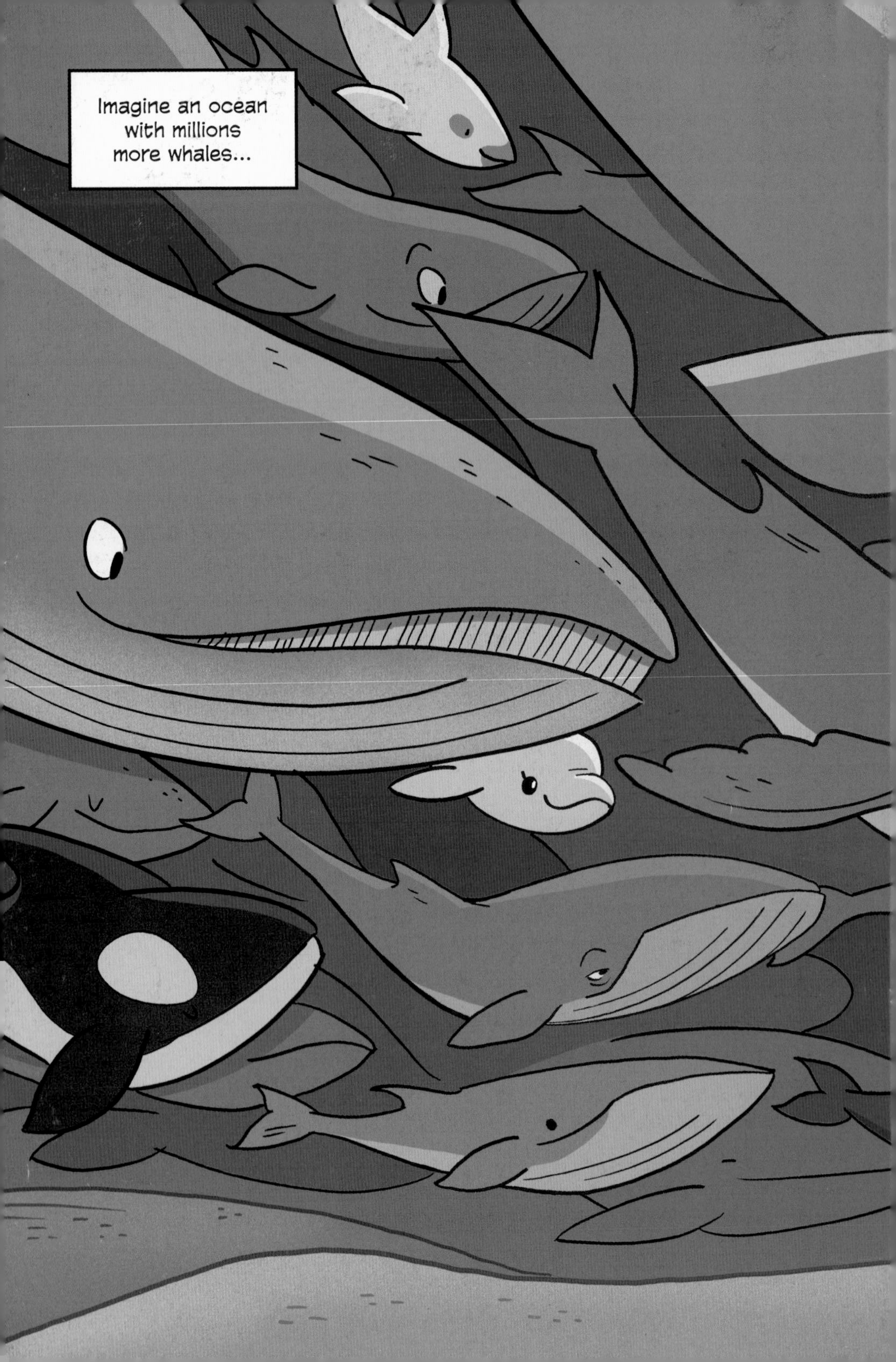
Imagine an ocean with millions more whales...

It was real just 100 years ago.

—NOTES—

Page 4
Zip is tagged with a DTAG, a tag attached to a whale using suction cups that contains a hydrophone (an underwater microphone) as well as a bunch of sensors that measure how a whale is moving and at what depth.

Page 6
Not all kinds of whales can make every type of sound; it depends on their unique anatomy and behaviors.

Page 8
"Pod" is the general term for a group of whales, though you will sometimes see "pod" used for Odontocetes and "herd" used for Mysticetes.

Page 18
Generally, the blow that we see is water vapor in the exhaled breath condensing, but if the blowhole is partly underwater, the exhaled air can push water above it into the blow as well.

Page 29
Very little is known about how Mysticetes locate prey patches. Some hypotheses, which are highlighted here, are built on the idea that they rely on a fuller range of their senses, but it is a hard idea to test!

Page 29
Lane's speech pattern is inspired by the gunshot vocalizations (short, loud bursts of sound characteristic of right whales).

Page 54
Not all carnivores, meat-eaters, are members of the order Carnivora, which is a taxonomic group (a specific evolutionary branch of animals). And not all members of the Carnivora are carnivores (think of pandas, which eat only bamboo). Confusing, I know.

Pages 84 & 85
Remember seasons happen at different times of the year in each hemisphere! When it is spring in the northern hemisphere, it is autumn in the southern hemisphere and vice versa!

Page 95
Teut has been following Zip this whole time out of curiosity, despite nearly getting eaten. Both Zip and Teut travel far outside their normal ranges for the sake of the story, but that's part of going on an adventure!

Page 109
Scientists have only recorded Cuvier's beaked whales making sounds during feeding so far, but the story depended on Zip talking to other whales, including those in his own pod. They have to maintain group cohesion somehow!

—FURTHER READING—

Cawardine, Mark (author), and Camm, Martin (illustrator). *DK Smithsonian Handbook of Whales, Dolphins, and Porpoises (2nd edition).* New York: Dorling Kindersley Publishing, 2002.

Lourie, Peter. *Whaling Season: A Year in the Life of an Arctic Whale Scientist (Reprint edition; Scientists in the Field Series).* New York: HMH Books for Young Readers, 2015.

Pyenson, Nick. *Spying on Whales: The Past, Present, and Future of Earth's Most Awesome Creatures.* New York: Penguin Random House, 2018.

Würsig, Bernd, Thewissen, J.G.M., and Kovacs, Kit. *Encyclopedia of Marine Mammals (3rd edition).* London: Academic Press, 2017.

Discovery of Sound in the Sea: https://dosits.org/.

Check out some science podcasts!
Brains On! Science Podcast for Kids
The Marine Mammal Science Podcast